No.1 for exam success

Verbal Reasoning

Assessment Papers

Challenge

9–10 years

OXFORD

UNIVERSITY PRESS

Great Clarendon Street, Oxford, OX2 6DP, United Kingdom

Oxford University Press is a department of the University of Oxford.
It furthers the University's objective of excellence in research,
scholarship, and education by publishing worldwide. Oxford is
a registered trade mark of Oxford University Press in the UK and in
certain other countries

First published in 2015
This edition published in 2021

British Library Cataloguing in Publication Data
Data available

978-0-19-277825-3

10 9 8 7 6 5 4 3 2 1

Paper used in the production of this book is a natural, recyclable
product made from wood grown in sustainable forests.
The manufacturing process conforms to the environmental
regulations of the country of origin.

Printed in China

Acknowledgements

The publishers would like to thank the following for permissions to
use copyright material:

Page make-up: OKS Prepress, India
Illustrations: OKS Prepress, India
Cover illustrations: Lo Cole

Although we have made every effort to trace and contact all
copyright holders before publication this has not been possible in all
cases. If notified, the publisher will rectify any errors or omissions at
the earliest opportunity.

Links to third party websites are provided by Oxford in good faith
and for information only. Oxford disclaims any responsibility for
the materials contained in any third party website referenced in
this work.

Introduction

What is Bond?

The Bond *Challenge* titles are the most stretching of the Bond assessment papers, the number one series for the 11+, selective exams and general practice. Bond *Challenge* is carefully designed to stretch above and beyond the level provided in the regular Bond assessment range.

How does this book work?

The book contains two distinct sets of papers, along with fully explained answers and a Progress Chart.

- Focus tests, accompanied by advice and directions, are focused on particular (and age-appropriate) verbal reasoning question types encountered in the 11+ and other exams, but devised at a higher level than the standard *Assessment Papers*. Each Focus test is designed to help raise a child's skills in the question type, as well as offer plenty of practice for the necessary techniques.

- Mixed papers are full-length tests containing a full range of verbal reasoning question types. These are designed to provide rigorous practice for children working at a level higher than that required to pass the 11+ and other verbal reasoning tests.

Fully explained answers are provided for both types of test in the middle of the book.

How much time should the tests take?

The tests are for practice and to reinforce learning, and you may wish to test exam techniques and working to a set time limit. Using the Mixed papers, we would recommend your child spends 40 minutes answering the 65 questions in each paper.

You can reduce the suggested time by five minutes to practise working at speed.

Using the Progress Chart

The Progress Chart can be used to track Focus test and Mixed paper results over time to monitor how well your child is doing and identify any repeated problems in tackling the different question types.

Focus test 1   Similars and opposites

Always read this type of question carefully, as most of them will have similar _and_ opposite options.

Underline the two words in each line that are most similar in type or meaning.

Example   <u>dear</u>   pleasant   poor   extravagant   <u>expensive</u>

Take care with words, like 'dear', that have more than one meaning.

1 <u>begin</u>   <u>finish</u>   <u>complete</u>   page   book   ✓

2 finger   tow   bell   <u>pull</u>   push   ✓ ✗

3 spare   <u>room</u>   bath   cooker   extra   ✗

1 **3**

Find a word that is <u>similar in</u> meaning to the word in capital letters and that rhymes with the second word.

Example   CABLE   tyre   <u>WIRE</u>

4 FIRM   card   _hard_

5 CAUTIOUS   dairy   _weary_

6 LIFT   gaze   _raze_ ✗
raise

If you cannot find a suitable similar word, try experimenting with rhyming words.

2 **3**

Work out the missing synonym. Spell the new word correctly, putting one letter in each space.

Example   strange   p e _ _ l _ _ r   (peculiar)

7 clever   I n t e l l i g e n t ✓

8 adequate   S a t i s f a c t o r y ✓

9 charming   f l a t t e r i n g ✗

10 shrewd   l e v e l - h e a d e d ✗

11 faint   i n d i s t i n c t

3 **5**

Underline the two words, one from each group, that are the most <u>opposite</u> in meaning.

Example   (dawn, <u>early</u>, wake)   (<u>late</u>, stop, sunrise)

12 (gentle, rough, <u>sea</u>)   (wave, <u>sand</u>, calm) ✗

13 (hit, <u>throw</u>, <u>ball</u>)   (thump, <u>catch</u>, stick) ✓

14 (speak, talk, <u>shout</u>)   (lie, truth, <u>whisper</u>) ✓   ② 3

Underline the two words, one from each group, that are the closest in meaning.

Example (race, shop, <u>start</u>)   (finish, <u>begin</u>, end)

15 (afternoon, morning, <u>noon</u>)   (midnight, <u>midday</u>, night) ✓

16 (sew, stitch, <u>mend</u>)   (break, <u>repair</u>, knit) ✓

17 (<u>gnaw</u>, tooth, fang)   (<u>chew</u>, claw, roar) ✓   ③ 3

Underline the pair of words most similar in meaning.

Example come, go   <u>roams, wanders</u>   fear, fare

18 divide, share   multiply, add   <u>borrow, steal</u> ✗

19 up, down   <u>on, in</u> ✗ below, under

20 hair, hare   <u>wash, rinse</u> ✓ look, find

21 pillow, duvet   cushion, chair   <u>carpet, rug</u> ✓   ② 4

> More than one pair of words may have similar meanings. Look for the most appropriate.

Underline the pair of words most opposite in meaning.

Example cup, mug   coffee, milk   <u>hot, cold</u>

22 clever, intelligent   <u>above, below</u> ✓ distant, far

23 neither, nor   for, four   <u>yes, no</u> ✓

24 huge, large   <u>immense, minute</u> ✓ broad, wide   ③ 3

Underline the word in the brackets closest in meaning to the word in capitals.

Example UNHAPPY (unkind   death   laughter   <u>sad</u>   friendly) ✓

25 ODD   (out   <u>peculiar</u>   polite   even   outside)

26 HIT   (miss   strike   goal   <u>punish</u>   kiss) ✗

27 SLACK   (taut   tight   quick   brief   <u>loose</u>) ✓   ② 3

Underline the one word in brackets that is most opposite in meaning to the word in capitals.

Example WIDE   (broad   vague   long   <u>narrow</u>   motorway)

28 STRAIGHT   (upright   even   fair   forward   <u>crooked</u>) ✓

29 CRY   (wail   <u>laugh</u> ✓ pity   tear   drop)

30 NEAR   (close   by   <u>far</u> ✓ there   here)   ③ 3

Focus test 2 — Sorting words

Look at these groups of words.

A	B	C
Animals	Colours	Transport

> Make sure you write the correct letter for each answer.

Choose the correct group for each of the words below. Write in the letter.

1–5 blue _B_   fox _A_   gerbil _A_   train _C_   kiwi _A_

bus _C_   turtle _A_   lorry _C_   yellow _B_   pink _B_

5

Underline the two words that are the odd ones out in the following group of words.

Example black   <u>king</u>   purple   green   <u>house</u>

6 rose   daisy   <u>sun</u>   <u>garden</u>   daffodil

7 <u>road</u>   lorry   bicycle   car   <u>bridge</u>

8 plunge   <u>hoist</u>   fall   <u>tumble</u>   elevate

9 weather   <u>spring</u>   autumn   <u>sunshine</u>   summer

4

Find and underline the two words that need to change places for each sentence to make sense.

Example She went to <u>letter</u> the <u>write</u>.

10 The party ended and it was <u>home</u> to go <u>time</u>.

11 The <u>wall</u> jumped gracefully onto the <u>cat</u>.

12 Please put <u>tidily</u> books away <u>your</u>.

> Always check the sense of the sentence carefully.

13 The <u>road</u> skidded on the icy <u>car</u>.

4

Underline the one word in the brackets that will go equally well with both pairs of words outside the brackets.

Example: cure, heal   gift, goodie   (sweet medicine doctor present <u>treat</u>)

This goes equally well with both pair of words because 'treat' can mean to give someone medical attention to try to make them better or a special item that gives pleasure.

14	third, first	hour, minute	(time second day fourth last)
15	omit, leave	caper, prance	(avoid skip hop trip ignore)
16	reasonable, just	pale, light	(honest soft subtle fair unbiased)
17	stone, slab	sway, swing	(tremble strength rock pillar roll)

4

Rearrange the muddled words in capital letters so that each sentence makes sense.

Example There are sixty SNODCES <u>seconds</u> in a UTMINE <u>minute</u>.

18 We crossed the road NGUIS _using_ the BRAZE _zebra_ crossing.

19 The pigeons ate the DREBA _bread_ we took to the RKAP _park_.

20 We lay in the long RSAGS _grass_ in the DLIEF _field_ after running our race.

21 The RTANI _Train_ was on time as it left the SNTAITO _Station_.

4

Underline the two words that are made from the same letters.

Example	TAP	PET	<u>TEA</u>	POT	<u>EAT</u>
22	<u>SPARE</u>	TEARS	<u>SPEAR</u>	PAIRS	PRESS
23	BREAK	<u>DREAD</u>	BREAD	<u>ADDER</u>	BRAID
24	HEALS	SHELL	SHALL	STALE	LEAST
25	<u>TREES</u>	TREAT	UTTER	<u>STEER</u>	TRUST

4

Rearrange the letters in capitals to make another word. The new word has something to do with the first two words or phrases.

Example	spot	soil	SAINT	<u>STAIN</u>
26	whiter	dimmer	PEARL	_paler_
27	soup	gruel	THROB	_broth_
28	orange	lime	MELON	_lemon_
29	frighten	shock	CARES	_scare_
30	fake	wrong	FLEAS	_false_

First look at the clues, then rearrange the letters to find the anagram.

5

Now go to the Progress Chart to record your score!   Total   **30**

Focus test 3 Selecting words

Complete the following sentences by selecting the most sensible word from each group of words given in the brackets. Underline the words selected.

Example   The (<u>children</u>, boxes, foxes) carried the (houses, <u>books</u>, steps) home from the (greengrocer, <u>library</u>, factory).

> Work through, bracket by bracket, and choose the most appropriate words.

1   The (scarecrow, <u>footballer</u>, vegetable) kicked the (can, <u>ball</u>, carrot) from one side of the (table, <u>pitch</u>, kitchen) to the other.

2   (<u>Yesterday</u>, Tomorrow, Next week) it rained and huge (balls, <u>puddles</u>, mirrors) covered the (<u>playground</u>, wall, film).

3   On Mother's (apron, <u>Day</u>, car), my father bought my (dog, brother, <u>mother</u>) a beautiful (book, <u>bunch</u>, crowd) of flowers.

4   She drove her (train, <u>car</u>, boat) down the (<u>road</u>, corridor, slide) and skidded on the (<u>ice</u>, pond, roof).

5   When you mix (<u>blue</u>, red, black) paint with (white, purple, <u>yellow</u>) paint, you make green (porridge, salad, <u>paint</u>).

Find two words, one from each set in brackets, that will complete the sentence in the most sensible way. Underline both words.

Example   Flea is to (fly, <u>flee</u>, insect) as bear is to (fur, dog, <u>bare</u>) because both are homophones of the preceding words in the sentence.

6   Flock is to (cows, horses, <u>sheep</u>) as herd is to (ducks, geese, <u>cows</u>).

7   Sing is to (voice, song, <u>sang</u>) as speak is to (quiet, talk, <u>spoke</u>).

8   Dishevelled is to (<u>neat</u>, special, messy) as wet is to (cold, <u>dry</u>, water).

9   Dangerous is to (<u>perilous</u>, accident, <u>safe</u>) as tranquil is to (lonely, pretty, <u>calm</u>).

10   Swan is to (chick, hen, <u>cygnet</u>) as goose is to (cub, <u>gosling</u>, gaggle).

Underline the one word in the brackets that will go equally well with both pairs of words outside the brackets.

Example   rush, attack   cost, fee   (price, hasten, strike, <u>charge</u>, money)

> Often each word in the brackets will go well with one pair of words. Sometimes the answer from the brackets has two very different meanings.

11	paste, glue	twig, wood	(tree, branch, tape, stick, adhere)
12	unripe, young	sickly, unwell	(green, red, black, brown, purple)
13	fib, falsehood	flat, recline	(truth, stand, lie, hide, even)
14	pale, faint	underweight, delicate	(skinny, thin, frail, dark, light)
15	crave, yearn	lengthy, tall	(high, hunger, wish, long, desire)

4 5

Underline two words, one from each group, that go together to form a new word. The word in the first group always comes first.

Example (hand, green, for)   (light, house, sure)

16	(card, letter, post)	(bell, board, van)
17	(rasp, red, flap)	(door, heart, berry)
18	(king, scare, black)	(crow, crown, row)
19	(shaving, tooth, pick)	(paste, cream, nice)
20	(hear, dirty, play)	(ground, ring, street)

> Take one word at a time from the left brackets and put it in front of each of the words in the right brackets.

4 5

Underline the one word in each group that **cannot be made** from the letters of the word in capital letters.

Example STATIONERY   stone   tyres   ration   nation   noisy

21	FEATHERS	shear	heath	trash	feast	sheer
22	CURTAINS	stain	trains	saint	trance	strain
23	KITCHENS	chins	stick	chick	kites	thick
24	FOOTBALLS	boots	float	stool	boast	frost
25	NOVEMBER	ember	remove	mover	eleven	venom

4 5

Underline the one word in each group that **can be made** from the letters of the word in capital letters.

Example CHAMPION   camping   notch   peach   cramp   chimp

26	SQUANDER	danger	queer	drain	queen	under
27	MASSAGES	message	games	grass	messes	chasm
28	SCRABBLE	bless	least	bleak	brash	clear
29	POSTMAN	stamen	nasty	spots	stamp	monster
30	FURNACES	creams	scared	surface	crust	snares

5 5

Now go to the Progress Chart to record your score!   Total 27 30

Focus test 4 Selecting letters

Which one letter can be added to the front of all of these words to make new words?

Example   __are   __at   __rate   __all   <u>c</u>

> Experiment with putting various letters in front of each of the words until you find the correct one.

1 __rifle   __ape   __otter   __ail   __

2 __ash   __hair   __lip   __art   __

3 __ear   __lack   __right   __less   __

4 __eat   __hoe   __tile   __tone   __

5 __east   __end   __ever   __adder   __

5

Find the letter that will end the first word and start the second word.

Example   drow (<u>n</u>) ought

6 brus (__) eight

7 foo (__) rail

8 garde (__) ote

9 mimi (__) loser

10 are (__) pples

> Look at the word on the left and find various letters that could finish that word. Then see which one you can also use to start the word on the right.

5

Find the letter that will complete both pairs of words, ending the first word and starting the second. The same letter must be used for both pairs of words.

Example   mea (<u>t</u>) able   fi (<u>t</u>) ub

11 shin (__) very   plat (__) ating

12 as (__) eys   quic (__) ettle

13 lam (__) est   com (__) ring

14 clif (__) airy   of (__) amous

15 hurr (__) east   pla (__) ear

> If you don't succeed with one pair, look at the other pair.

5

Move one letter from the first word and add it to the second word to make two new words.

Example hunt sip <u>hut</u> <u>snip</u>

> Take one letter at a time from the first word and see if you can make a new word. Then place the letter into the second word until you have made a proper word.

16	dwell	span	_____	_____
17	blame	rave	_____	_____
18	tangle	mean	_____	_____
19	wash	wine	_____	_____
20	stroke	age	_____	_____

5

Add one letter to the word in capital letters to make a new word. The meaning of the new word is given in the clue.

> Add suitable letters to the word in capitals and think about the meaning to help you. Alternatively, look at the meaning and find a word that uses the word in capitals.

Example PLAN simple <u>PLAIN</u>

21	FOND	discovered	_____
22	YARN	long for	_____
23	CARTON	film made from drawings	_____
24	ANGER	peril	_____
25	BOTHER	a close relation	_____

5

Remove one letter from the word in capital letters to leave a new word. The meaning of the new word is given in the clue.

> Here, you need to take a letter away rather than add one.

Example AUNT an insect <u>ANT</u>

26	CLIMB	leg or arm	_____
27	CHASE	a container	_____
28	FLOUR	a number	_____
29	FIRST	clenched hand	_____
30	STRING	a bee's weapon	_____

5

Change one word so that the sentence makes sense. Underline the word you are taking out and write your new word on the line.

Example I waited in line to buy a <u>book</u> to see the film.   <u>ticket</u>

1 Our cat carried my brother with her sharp claws.   _____

2 My mother plaited my coat as it had grown so long.   _____

3 The referee blew his ball loudly so everyone could hear it.   _____

4 The choir climbed the song tunefully and musically.   _____   (4

Find the three-letter word that can be added to the letters in capitals to make a new word. The new word will complete the sentence sensibly. Write the three-letter word.

Example The cat sprang onto the MO.   <u>USE</u>

5 Mary closed the garden G behind her.   _____

6 The queen wore a golden CN covered with jewels.   _____

7 The WHS span on the icy road.   _____

8 When I broke my arm I had to go to HOSAL for an X-ray.   _____   (4

Find a word that can be put in front of each of the following words to make new, compound words.

Example	cast	fall	ward	pour	<u>down</u>	
9	writing	some	cuff	book	_____	
10	song	watch	cage	seed	_____	
11	land	lighter	way	brow	_____	
12	power	work	break	cracker	_____	
13	bowl	cake	net	tail	_____	(5

> Look for common words such as up/down, black/white, on/in.

Change the first word of the third pair in the same way as the other pairs to give a new word.

Example bind, hind   bare, hare   but, <u>hut</u>

14 tool, too   feel, fee   beer, _____

15 put, pat   bun, ban   fur, _____

16 war, raw   dab, bad   rat, _____

17 stale, ale   flown, own   charm, _____

4

Find the four-letter word hidden at the end of one word and the beginning of the next word in each sentence. The order of the letters may not be changed.

Example   We had bat<u>s and</u> balls.   <u>sand</u>

  18 We are going to the cinema later today.   _____

  19 I am travelling in this car.   _____

  20 The clown made us laugh and laugh.   _____

  21 The horse jumped over the gate.   _____

4

Look at the first group of three words. The word in the middle has been made from the two other words. Complete the second group of three words in the same way, making a new word in the middle of the group.

Example   PA<u>IN</u>   INTO   <u>TO</u>OK   ALSO   <u>SOON</u>   ONLY

> Letter by letter, see where the middle word in the first group gets its letters from. Repeat the pattern for the second group of words.

  22 CASH   SHOP   OPEN   PAID   _____   LENT

  23 HATE   HANG   SUNG   CLUE   _____   WRAP

  24 POOR   BOOK   BEAK   FOUR   _____   SLIP

  25 WING   SING   SOCK   PART   _____   CLUE

4

Change the first word into the last word by changing one letter at a time and making a new, different word in the middle.

Example   CASE   <u>CASH</u>   LASH

  26 HARK   _____   WARD

  27 POOR   _____   FOUR

  28 BEAM   _____   HEAD

  29 FISH   _____   WASH

  30 MINT   _____   FIST

> Write down the letters that remain the same. Substitute the remaining letters one at a time.

5

Now go to the Progress Chart to record your score!   Total   30

Focus test 6　Substitution and logic

If a = 3, b = 2, c = 6, d = 5 and e = 1, find the value of the following calculations.

> Replace the letters with numbers and work out the calculations.

Using the same values, write the answers as a letter.

1　c − d = _____　　　　　　**2**　a − e = _____

3　c ÷ b = _____　　　　　　**4**　d − b = _____

5　(b − e) × d = _____　　　**6**　(d + a) − b = _____

7　(ab) ÷ c = _____

7

If e = 3, l = 1, m = 4, i = 2 and s = 7, what are the totals of these words?

8　lies　_____　　　　**9**　lime　_____　　　　**10**　smile　_____

3

Read the first two statements and then underline one of the four options below that must be true.

11　Her pencils are sharp. All of her pencils are red.

　　A My pencil is blunt.　　　　　**B** All her red pencils are sharp.

　　C All pencils in the world are sharp.　　**D** Red pencils are always sharp.

12　Some houses are made of bricks. All houses have roofs.

　　A Houses are not made of stone.　　**B** Some houses have chimneys.

　　C We have a wooden front door.　　**D** Brick houses have roofs.

2

Four friends, A, B, C, and D, like different colours. C and D like red. The other two like yellow. A and D like green. B's favourite colour is yellow but she dislikes red. All of them like blue except D.

13　Which is the most popular colour?　_____

14　Who likes red as well as green?　_____

15　Who likes three colours?　_____

3

　　LEEDS　　HUDDERSFIELD　　CROYDON　　YORK　　READING

If these towns are put into alphabetical order, which comes:

16　first?　_____

17　last?　_____

> Write the words in alphabetical order before you begin.

18　fourth?　_____

A B C D E F G H I J K L M N O P Q R S T U V W X Y Z

If the days of the week are put into alphabetical order, which comes:

19 first? _____

20 last? _____

5

This is a diagram of six school lockers. A and E have already been taken.

TOP

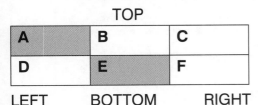

LEFT   BOTTOM   RIGHT

> Write down the children's names. Read each sentence carefully and write down, next to their names, who has which locker using the given information.

Mo took a locker on the top level. Angie took one on the bottom level but not directly under Mo's. Fern's was somewhere to the left of Greg's. He was on the same level as Mo. Which locker did each child take?

21 Mo _____   **22** Fern _____   **23** Angie _____   **24** Greg _____

4

Using the picture below, select the correct compass points in the questions.

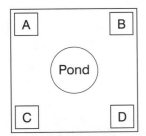
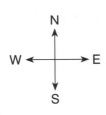

> Use the compass points to help you.

25 House A is to the (west, north, east) of House B. _____

26 House D is to the (east, north, south) of House B. _____

27 The pond is (south-west, south-east, north-west) of House A. _____

3

May is four years younger than her sister, Bess, who in turn is twice her little brother, Tom's, age. Sarah, their mother, was 26 when May was born. She is now 32. How old are the children?

28 May _____   **29** Bess _____   **30** Tom _____

3

Now go to the Progress Chart to record your score!   Total   30

15

The code for CREAMS is 4 8 0 2 9 5. Encode each of these words using the same code.

> First line up the code with the word: C R E A M S
>   4 8 0 2 9 5
>
> Then substitute the letters for numbers.

1 RACE _____   **2** SAME _____

Decode these words using the same code as above.

3 5 0 0 9 _____   **4** 2 8 0 2 _____   **4**

The code for STABLE is ← ↓ → ↘ ↕ ↑. Encode each of these words using the same code.

5 BALE _____   **6** SALT _____

Decode these words using the same code as above.

7 ↕ → ← ↓ _____   **8** → ↘ ↕ ↑ _____   **4**

Match the right word to each code given below.

   PLAY   YARD   PEEL   LEAP

> Look for letters that stand out. Here, two words begin with P, and one word has a double E.

9 w k z o _____   **10** s m k u _____

11 u m m s _____   **12** u s k w _____

13 Using the same code, decode z m k s. _____   **5**

14 If the code for HOLLOW is 4 9 6 6 9 2, what is the code for WOOL? _____

15 Using the same code, decode 4 9 2 6. _____

16 If the code for SPEARS is ? & % @ ! ?, encode PASS. _____

17 Using the same code, decode & % @ !. _____

18 If the code for STRING is F X Z B V O, encode GRIN. _____

19 Using the same code, decode X B V F. _____

Make sure you write down the code accurately.

20 If the code for FASTER is B c 5 k ^ /, what is the code for STAR? _____

21 Using the same code, decode B ^ c /. _____

8

A B C D E F G H I J K L M N O P Q R S T U V W X Y Z

Example If the code for CAT is D B U, what is the code for DOG? <u>E P H</u>

Look at the relationship of each of the letters with its code. Here, the code for C is D, the next letter in the alphabet. Check that the others follow the same pattern.

22 If the code for DESK is E F T L, what is the code for FAME? _____

23 If the code for LEFT is M F G U, what is the code for BARN? _____

24 If the code for BITE is A H S D, what is the code for LOOK? _____

25 If the code for NOTE is M N S D, what is the code for WILD? _____

26 If the code for COMB is E Q O D, what is the code for HAIR? _____

27 If the code for FORK is G P S L, what is T P J M? _____

28 If the code for SAIL is T B J M, what is Q P S U? _____

29 If the code for DUST is C T R S, what is E H Q L? _____

30 If the code for BEAR is D G C T, what is E W D U? _____

9

Complete the following sentences in the best way by choosing one word from each set of brackets.

Example　Tall is to (tree, <u>short</u>, colour) as narrow is to (thin, white, <u>wide</u>).

> Look for the relationship between the pairs of statements. Here it is opposites. The second pairing must be completed in the same way.
>
> Look carefully as sometimes there appears to be more than one answer.

1　High is to low as (big, cool, behind) is to (small, dirty, blue).

2　Dog is to (collar, bone, paw) as (horse, bird, lion) is to hoof.

3　Smile is to (toes, mouth, arm) as listen is to (ears, heart, fingers).

4　(Bed, garden, tractor) is to (window, water, pillow) as chair is to cushion.

5　Head is to (brains, hat, hair) as (foot, toenail, nose) is to sock.

6　(Hard, Easy, Moving) is to difficult as (wide, upset, throw) is to broad.

6

Fill in the missing letters. The alphabet has been written out to help you.

A B C D E F G H I J K L M N O P Q R S T U V W X Y Z

Example　AB is to CD as PQ is to <u>RS</u>.

> Look for the pattern. In these, both letters are working together.
>
> (It may help to put your finger on the alphabet line and count the number of spaces.)

7　QR is to ST as UV is to ___.

8　VW is to XY as KL is to ___.

9　AC is to EG as NP is to ___.

10　DE is to EF as FG is to ___.

11　ZY is to XW as VU is to ___.

12　AA is to DD as GG is to ___.

6

Give the two missing pairs of letters in the following sequences. The alphabet has been written out for you.

A B C D E F G H I J K L M N O P Q R S T U V W X Y Z

Example   CQ   DP   EQ   FP   <u>GQ</u>   <u>HP</u>

See whether the letters are working together or independently, as in the example.

13	EF	GH	___	___	MN	
14	Zy	___	Vu	Ts	___	
15	___	EG	IK	MO	___	
16	XF	YG	XH	___	___	YK
17	BI	___	___	EL	FM	GN
18	___	KE	LD	___	NB	OA
19	ZB	YD	___	WH	VJ	___
20	Hi3	Jk4	Lm5	No6	___	___

⟋ 8

Example   RS   TU   VW   XY   <u>ZA</u>   <u>BC</u>

21	UV	WX	___	___	CD	EF
22	___	CB	___	YX	WV	UT
23	YZ	SA	___	___	YD	SE

When you reach the end of the alphabet, treat it like a continuous line – XYZAB and BAZYX, and so on.

⟋ 3

Give the two missing numbers in the following sequences.

Example   2   4   6   8   <u>10</u>   <u>12</u>

24	24	21	___	15	12	___
25	___	___	27	37	47	57
26	1	5	___	13	___	21
27	55	45	35	___	___	5
28	2	___	8	___	32	64
29	66	3	66	4	___	___
30	3	4	6	9	___	___

Look for the pattern between the numbers.

Sometimes, the increase/decrease is irregular.

⟋ 7

Mixed paper 1

Underline the two words in each line that are most similar in type or meaning.

Example	dear	pleasant	poor	extravagant	expensive
1	flat	palace	level	heavy	light
2	grin	mutter	shout	frown	mumble
3	calm	boil	shiny	bright	sad
4	distant	near	far	way	view
5	sun	wind	carve	twist	meat

5

Underline the one word in each group that **can be made** from the letters of the word in capital letters.

Example	CHAMPION	camping	notch	peach	cramp	chimp
6	CRINKLES	chick	skirt	links	crack	scale
7	BRAVERY	zebra	berry	every	slave	really
8	CURIOUS	scour	curry	riots	sauce	sorry
9	MURDERS	dress	drums	medal	rudder	summer
10	PITCHES	stitch	cheese	cheap	clips	spice

5

Look at these groups of words.

A	B	C
Animals	Stationery	Rooms

Choose the correct group for each of the words below. Write in the letter.

11–15 horse ___   bedroom ___   pencil ___   kitchen ___   rabbit ___

  wolf ___   sharpener ___   bathroom ___   cheetah ___   rubber ___

5

Change one word so that the sentence makes sense. Underline the word you are taking out and write your new word on the line.

Example   I waited in line to buy a <u>book</u> to see the film.   <u>ticket</u>

16   During the night, clouds fell and our garden was white.   _____

17   At the restaurant, the waiter opened a box of wine with the corkscrew.   _____

18   Sam gave his cat a bone after taking him for a walk in the park.   _____

19   The television rang and my mother answered it.   _____

20   A robin is a garden gnome with a red breast.   _____   **5**

Find the letter that will end the first word and start the second word.

Example   drow (<u>n</u>) ought

21   biscui (__) erm   **22**   donke (__) ard

23   lan (__) ragon   **24**   pil (__) nough

25   clif (__) orest   **5**

Match the right word to each code given below.

     FLAP   FOOL   FLAN   OPEN

26   8 6 6 9   _____   **27**   6 7 4 3   _____

28   8 9 1 3   _____   **29**   8 9 1 7   _____

30   Using the same code, decode 7 1 3 4.   _____   **5**

Find the three-letter word that can be added to the letters in capitals to make a new word. The new word will complete the sentence sensibly. Write the three-letter word.

Example   The cat sprang onto the MO.   <u>USE</u>

31   Do up all the TONS on your shirt.   _____

32   Headlines in SPAPERS are usually in capitals.   _____

33   Cars travel on roads, people walk on PAVETS.   _____

34   Edinburgh is the capital of SCOTL.   _____

35   The grass on our garden N needs mowing.   _____   **5**

Add one letter to the word in capital letters to make a new word. The meaning of the new word is given in the clue.

Example PLAN   simple   <u>PLAIN</u>

36   PUMP   rounded   _____

37   HAIR   a seat   _____

38   STUCK   hit   _____

39   TART   begin   _____

40   LEVER   intelligent   _____   **5**

Underline the two words, one from each group, that are the most opposite in meaning.

Example   (dawn, <u>early</u>, wake)   (<u>late</u>, stop, sunrise)

41   (supple, inflexible, coherent)   (pliable, strong, clear)

42   (combine, part, reaper)   (harvester, solidify, separate)

43   (ascend, plunge, hurtle)   (dash, plod, extract)

44   (craven, constant, circular)   (timid, fearful, bold)

45   (uproar, optimistic, upstage)   (downhill, downsize, downbeat)   **5**

Underline the two words that are the odd ones out in the following group of words.

Example   black   <u>king</u>   purple   green   <u>house</u>

46   abundant   meagre   sparse   scanty   placid

47   dutiful   obedient   truthful   penitent   compliant

48   tow   haul   shove   push   pull

49   scramble   poach   confuse   peril   jumble

50   sagging   slack   taut   limp   negligent   **5**

If a = 1, b = 5, c = 3, d = 2 and e = 10, work out the answers to these. Write your answer as a letter.

51 $e - (b + c) =$ _____

52 $b + c + d =$ _____

53 $bd =$ _____

54 $e \div d =$ _____

55 $(e - c) - (c + a) =$ _____

5

Complete the following sentences in the best way by choosing one word from each set of brackets.

Example Tall is to (tree, <u>short</u>, colour) as narrow is to (thin, white, <u>wide</u>).

56 Query is to (question, response, ask) as problem is to (solution, necessity, mixture).

57 Silhouette is to (outsider, outlay, outline) as crisis is to (pronouncement, pirouette, predicament).

58 Tepid is to (icy, lukewarm, brittle) as half-hearted is to (wholehearted, apathetic, fragile).

59 Finger is to (toe, hand, nail) as ankle is to (thigh, shoulder, wrist).

60 Decline is to (accept, refuse, partake) as despise is to (respect, condone, distend).

5

Underline two words, one from each group, that go together to form a new word. The word in the first group always comes first.

Example (hand, <u>green</u>, for)   (light, <u>house</u>, sure)

61 (break, mend, stilt)   (age, term, bottle)

62 (news, garden, avail)   (gate, able, town)

63 (dark, light, big)   (night, noon, house)

64 (pink, high, grape)   (lights, hill, bag)

65 (two, ten, nine)   (lives, or, time)

5

Mixed paper 2

Fill in the crosswords so that all the given words are included. You have been given one letter as a clue in each crossword.

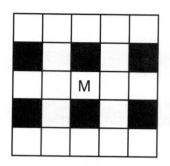

1

GAMES

DREAM

STATE

ALERT

ROAST

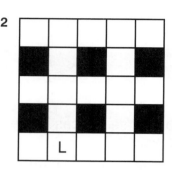

2

FLARE

INNER

BRAIN

SPINE

REPEL

2

Change the first word of the third pair in the same way as the other pairs to give a new word.

Example   bind, hind   bare, hare   but, <u>hut</u>

3   tin, tan   rim, ram   hit, _____

4   ran, rook   bit, book   car, _____

5   butter, but   bargain, bar   business, _____

3

Find a word that is similar in meaning to the word in capital letters and that rhymes with the second word.

Example   CABLE   tyre   <u>WIRE</u>

6   JUMP   sleep   _____

7   GROUND   birth   _____

8   WEALTHY   ditch   _____

9   IMITATE   sloppy   _____

10   PRIOR   floor   _____

5

Complete the following sentences by selecting the most sensible word from each group of words given in the brackets. Underline the words selected.

Example   The (<u>children</u>, boxes, foxes) carried the (houses, <u>books</u>, steps) home from the (greengrocer, <u>library</u>, factory).

11   We had (children, computers, sausages), (flowers, chips, moles) and (boats, beans, books) for school lunch today.

12   (Two, Sixty, Forty-four) plus (six, ten, three) equals (five, four, three).

13   My reading (arm, book, station) has one hundred (ants, currants, pages) and it is really (exciting, chilly, damp).

14   We have a nest of baby (elephants, birds, dinosaurs) in our (lorry, fireworks, garden) hedge that the parents are constantly (talking, beating, feeding).

15   We have recycling (bins, balloons, ponds) at the back of the (playground, sky, stool) at (ceiling, school, the sea).

5

Find the letter that will complete both pairs of words, ending the first word and starting the second. The same letter must be used for both pairs of words.

Example   mea (<u>t</u>) able   fi (<u>t</u>) ub

16   crac (__) ing   stoc (__) ipper

17   ro (__) erry   cra (__) ox

18   stra (__) et   willo (__) ant

19   baske (__) op   kni (__) error

20   hai (__) et   cal (__) emon

5

GREEN   GREY   RED   BLUE   YELLOW

If these colours are put into alphabetical order, which comes:

21   second?   _____

22   third?   _____

23   fourth?   _____

3

25

Read the first two statements and then underline one of the four options below that must be true.

24 Beetles are insects. Some beetles have wings.

    A All beetles are insects.   **B** All beetles have wings.

    C Winged insects bite.   **D** All insects are beetles.

25 James is a boy's name. All boys have names.

    A All boys are called James.   **B** James is a girl's name.

    C Every boy has a brother called   **D** Some boys are called James.
        James.

2

If the code for PARENTS is □ ÷ ◊ △ ○ ● △, decode:

26 □ △ ÷ ◊ _____   27 ● ◊ ÷ □ _____

28 △ ● ÷ ◊ _____   29 ○ △ △ ● _____

30 ● ◊ △ △ _____

5

Find a word that can be put in front of each of the following words to make new, compound words.

Example	cast	fall	ward	pour	<u>down</u>
31	stairs	stream	hill	on	_____
32	hear	grown	board	night	_____
33	berry	board	bird	currant	_____
34	ball	drop	flake	plough	_____
35	fall	colour	ski	proof	_____

5

Move one letter from the first word and add it to the second word to make two new words.

Example	hunt	sip	<u>hut</u>	<u>snip</u>
36	brain	ramble	_____	_____
37	glove	ate	_____	_____
38	there	sick	_____	_____
39	grown	fill	_____	_____
40	trickle	spot	_____	_____

5

Focus test 1: Similars and Opposites (pages 4–5)

1 **finish, complete** To 'finish' or 'complete' something means to end it.
2 **tow, pull** Both 'tow' and 'pull' mean to drag.
3 **spare, extra** Both 'spare' and 'extra' imply there is more left over.
4 **HARD** 'Firm' and 'hard' are both adjectives to describe something that has a solid or rigid structure and is not easy to break.
5 **WARY** 'Cautious' and 'wary' are both adjectives that describe the state of being careful or alert to danger.
6 **RAISE** 'Lift' and 'raise' both mean to move something up to a higher level.
7 **intelligent** Both words mean smart, quick-witted and astute.
8 **satisfactory** Both words mean acceptable or sufficient.
9 **flattering** Both words mean complimenting or saying nice things to someone.
10 **level-headed** Both words mean sensible or rational.
11 **indistinct** Both words mean vague in appearance or hard to make out.
12 **rough, calm** Referring to the sea, a 'rough' sea is when the waves are big. If it is 'calm' the waves are small.
13 **throw, catch** When you 'throw' a ball you are sending it away from yourself. You 'catch' it when the ball comes to you.
14 **shout, whisper** A 'shout' is loud whereas a 'whisper' is very quiet.
15 **noon, midday** 'Noon' and 'midday' are both words meaning 12:00pm.
16 **mend, repair** 'Mend' and 'repair' both mean to fix, patch up or refurbish.
17 **gnaw, chew** Both words refer to actions of the mouth whilst eating food.
18 **divide, share** Both words mean to split something up or to distribute something.
19 **below, under** Both words are prepositions showing that something is beneath another object.
20 **wash, rinse** Both words refer to cleaning using water.
21 **carpet, rug** Both words are coverings for the floor.
22 **above, below** 'Above' means over whereas 'below' means under.
23 **yes, no** 'Yes' is affirmative whereas 'no' is negative.
24 **immense, minute** 'Immense' means vast whereas 'minute' means very small.
25 **peculiar** Both 'odd' and 'peculiar' mean strange or irregular.
26 **strike** Both 'hit' and 'strike' mean to thump or collide with.
27 **loose** Both 'slack' and 'loose' mean sagging or floppy.
28 **crooked** 'Straight' is upright whereas 'crooked' is bent.
29 **laugh** To 'cry' is to wail whereas to 'laugh' is to giggle.
30 **far** 'Near' is close by whereas 'far' is a long way away.

Focus test 2: Sorting words (pages 6–7)

1–5 **A: fox, gerbil, kiwi, turtle** These are all animals.
  B: blue, yellow, pink These are all colours.
  C: train, bus, lorry These are all forms of transport.
6 **sun, garden** The other words are all flowers.
7 **road, bridge** The other words are all forms of transport.
8 **hoist, elevate** The other words are related to going downwards.
9 **weather, sunshine** The other words are all seasons.
10 The party ended and it was **time** to go **home**.
11 The **cat** jumped gracefully onto the **wall**.
12 Please put **your** books away **tidily**.
13 The **car** skidded on the icy **road**.
14 **second** 'Third' and 'first' refer to numerical order as does 'second'; 'hour', 'minute' and 'second' are all units of time.
15 **skip** 'Omit', 'leave' and 'skip' can all mean to miss something out; 'skip' can also mean to move in along lightly, as do 'caper' and 'prance'.
16 **fair** 'Reasonable' and 'just' mean something or someone is treated equally and without prejudice, as does 'fair'; 'fair' can also refer to something 'pale' or 'light', often hair or complexion.
17 **rock** 'Rock', 'slab' or 'stone' all refer to a solid piece of a mineral material; 'rock', 'sway' or 'swing' can also mean to gently move something side to side.
18 **using, zebra**   19 **bread, park**
20 **grass, field**   21 **train, station**
22 **SPARE, SPEAR**   23 **DREAD, ADDER**
24 **STALE, LEAST**   25 **TREES, STEER**
26 **PALER**   27 **BROTH**
28 **LEMON**   29 **SCARE**
30 **FALSE**

Bond Verbal Reasoning Assessment Papers Challenge 9–10 years

Focus test 3: Selecting words
(pages 8–9)

1–5 Try each of the words in the first set of brackets. Do they make sense with any words in the second and third set of brackets? Only one combination of three words makes sense. It can also be useful to look at the tense of the verb in the sentence, for example a past tense verb cannot be used to refer to 'tomorrow'.

1 **footballer, ball, pitch**
2 **Yesterday, puddles, playground**
3 **Day, mother, bunch**
4 **car, road, ice**
5 **blue, yellow, paint**
6 **sheep, cows** They relate to the collective nouns that precede them in the sentence; 'flock' is the collective noun for sheep and 'herd' is the collective noun for cows.
7 **sang, spoke** Both are the past tense of the verb preceding them.
8 **neat, dry** They are both opposites to the words preceding them; 'dishevelled' and 'neat' are opposites and 'wet' and 'dry' are opposites.
9 **perilous, calm** Both are synonyms for the words preceding them in the sentence; 'dangerous' and perilous' are synonyms and 'tranquil' and 'calm' are synonyms.
10 **cygnet, gosling** Both are the word for the baby of the animal preceding it in the sentence.
11 **stick** To 'paste' or 'glue' is to 'stick' something together; a 'twig' or bit of 'wood' is referred to as a 'stick'.
12 **green** An 'unripe' or 'young' banana is 'green'; if you are feeling a bit 'green' you are 'sickly' or 'unwell'.
13 **lie** A 'lie' is an untruth or 'fib' or 'falsehood'; to 'lie' down is to be 'flat' or 'recline'.
14 **light** If a colour is 'pale' or 'faint' it is said to be 'light'; 'light' is also used to describe something that is 'underweight' or 'delicate'.
15 **long** If you 'crave' or 'yearn' for something, you desire it or 'long' for it; 'long' is also the opposite of short and means the same as 'lengthy' or 'tall'.
16–20 Remember the new word you make must be a compound word, not two separate words that can form a noun phrase such as 'shaving cream'.
16 **cardboard**   17 **raspberry**
18 **scarecrow**   19 **toothpaste**
20 **playground**
21 **heath** There is only one 'h' in 'FEATHERS'.
22 **trance** There is no 'e' in 'CURTAINS'.

23 **chick** There is only one 'c' in 'KITCHENS'.
24 **frost** There is no 'r' in 'FOOTBALLS'.
25 **eleven** There is no 'l' and only two 'e's in 'NOVEMBER'.
26 **under**   27 **games**   28 **clear**
29 **stamp**   30 **surface**

Focus test 4: Selecting letters
(pages 10–11)

1 **t** trifle, tape, totter, tail
2 **c** cash, chair, clip, cart
3 **b** bear, black, bright, bless
4 **s** seat, shoe, stile, stone
5 **l** least, lend, lever, ladder
6 **h** brush, height
7 **t** foot, trail
8 **n** garden, note
9 **c** mimic, closer
10 **a** area, apples
11 **e** shine, every; plate, eating
12 **k** ask, keys; quick, kettle
13 **b** lamb, best; comb, bring
14 **f** cliff, fairy; off, famous
15 **y** hurry, yeast; play, year
16 **w** dell, spawn
17 **b** lame, brave
18 **t** angle, meant
19 **h** was, whine
20 **r** stoke, rage
21 **FOUND**   22 **YEARN**
23 **CARTOON**   24 **DANGER**
25 **BROTHER**   26 **LIMB**
27 **CASE**   28 **FOUR**
29 **FIST**   30 **STING**

Focus test 5: Finding words
(pages 12–13)

1 **carried, scratched** Our cat scratched my brother with her sharp claws.
2 **coat, hair** My mother plaited my hair as it had grown so long.
3 **ball, whistle** The referee blew his whistle loudly so everyone could hear it.
4 **climbed, sang** The choir sang the song tunefully and musically.
5 **ATE** gate
6 **ROW** crown
7 **EEL** wheels
8 **PIT** hospital
9 **hand** handwriting, handsome, handcuff, handbook
10 **bird** birdsong, birdwatch, birdcage, birdseed
11 **high** highland, highlighter, highway, highbrow
12 **fire** firepower, firework, firebreak, firecracker

A2

13 **fish** fishbowl, fishcake, fishnet, fishtail
14 **bee** The pattern is to remove the final letter from the first word.
15 **far** The pattern is to change the second letter from 'u' to 'a'.
16 **tar** The pattern is to reverse the letters in the first word.
17 **arm** The pattern is to remove the first two letters.
18 **Wear** <u>We ar</u>e going to the cinema today.
19 **scar** I am travelling in thi<u>s car</u>.
20 **hand** The clown made us laug<u>h and</u> laugh.
21 **dove** The horse jump<u>ed ove</u>r the gate.
22–23 Use grids as shown below to help work out the missing word.
22 **IDLE**

		1	2		3	4	
C	A	S	H		O	P	E	N

		1	2		3	4	
P	A	I	D		L	E	N	T

23 **CLAP**

1	2					3	4
H	A	T	E		S	U	N	G

1	2					3	4
C	L	U	E		W	R	A	P

24 **SOUP**

	2/3	2/3			1			4
P	O	O	R		B	E	A	K

	2/3	2/3			1			4
F	O	U	R		S	L	I	P

25 **CART**

	2	3	4		1			
W	I	N	G		S	O	C	K

	2	3	4		1			
P	A	R	T		C	L	U	E

26 **HARD**   27 **POUR**
28 **BEAD**   29 **WISH**
30 **MIST**

Focus test 6: Substitution and logic (pages 14–15)

1 **e** 6 − 5 = 1
2 **b** 3 − 1 = 2
3 **a** 6 ÷ 2 = 3
4 **a** 5 − 2 = 3
5 **d** (2 − 1) × 5 = 5
6 **c** (5 + 3) − 2 = 6; 6 = c
7 **e** (3 × 2) ÷ 6 = 1; 1 = e
8 **13** 1 + 2 + 3 + 7 = 13
9 **10** 1 + 2 + 4 + 3 = 10
10 **17** 7 + 4 + 2 + 1 + 3 = 17
11 **B** You must use only the information you are given. A, C and D may or may not be true. B

refers directly to 'her' and the facts that all her pencils are red and sharp.
12 **D** You must use only the information you are given. A, B and C may or may not be true. Only 'Brick houses must have roofs' must be true in this case.
13–15 Use a grid to help you sort the information.

	red	yellow	green	blue
A		✓	✓	✓
B	✗	✓		✓
C	✓			✓
D	✓		✓	

13 **blue**   14 **D**   15 **A**
16–18 Use a grid to help you.

C	R	O	Y	D	O	N					1st
H	U	D	D	E	R	S	F	I	E	L	D	2nd
L	E	E	D	S							3rd
R	E	A	D	I	N	G					4th
Y	O	R	K								5th

16 **CROYDON**   17 **YORK**
18 **READING**
19–20 Use a grid to help you.

F	R	I	D	A	Y			1st
M	O	N	D	A	Y			2nd
S	A	T	U	R	D	A	Y	3rd
S	U	N	D	A	Y			4th
T	H	U	R	S	D	A	Y	5th
T	U	E	S	D	A	Y		6th
W	E	D	N	E	S	D	A	Y	7th

19 **Friday**   20 **Wednesday**
21–24 Use a grid to help you.

MO	B/C
FERN	B/D
ANGIE	D/F
GREG	B/C

Because Mo and Greg are on the top level, Angie must be F and Fern D. As Mo is not directly above Angie (F), he must be B and Greg is C.
21 **B**   23 **F**
22 **D**   24 **C**
25 **west**   26 **south**
27 **south-east**
28–30 If the mother, Sarah, was 26 when May was born, and is now 32, May must be 32 − 26 = 6. May is 4 years younger than Bess so Bess is 6 + 4 = 10. Bess is twice Tom's age so Tom must be 10 ÷ 2 = 5.
28 **6**   29 **10**   30 **5**

Focus test 7: Codes (pages 16–17)

1 **8240** R = 8, A = 2, C = 4, E = 0
2 **5290** S = 5, A = 2, M = 9, E = 0
3 **SEEM** 5 = S, 0 = E, 0 = E, 9 = M

Bond Verbal Reasoning Assessment Papers Challenge 9–10 years

4 **AREA** 2 = A, 8 = R, 0 = E, 2 = A

5–8 Use a grid to help you.

←	↓	→	↘	↕	↑
S	T	A	B	L	E

5 ↘ → ↕ ↑ B = ↘, A = →, L = ↕, E = ↑

6 ← → ↕ ↓ S = ←, A = →, L = ↕, T = ↓

7 **LAST** ↕ = L, → = A, ← = S, ↓ = T

8 **ABLE** → = A, ↘ = B, ↕ = L, ↑ = E

9–13 Two of the words start with 'P', so 'P' = 'u'. 'PEEL' must be 'u m m s' because of the double 'e'. From this information, you can work out all the code letters.

9 **YARD** w = Y, k = A, z = R, o = D

10 **LEAP** s = L, m = E, k = A, u = P

11 **PEEL** u = P, m = E, m = E, s = L

12 **PLAY** u = P, s = L, k = A, w = Y

13 **REAL** z = R, m = E, k = A, s = L

14 **2996** W = 2, O = 9, O = 9, L = 6

15 **HOWL** 4 = H, 9 = O, 2 = W, 6 = L

16 **& @ ? ?** P = &, A = @, S = ?, S = ?

17 **PEAR** & = P, % = E, @ = A, ! = R

18 **O Z B V** G = O, R = Z, I = B, N = V

19 **TINS** X = T, B = I, V = N, F = S

20 **5 k c /** S = 5, T = k, A = c, R = /

21 **FEAR** B = F, ^ = E, c = A, / = R

22–30 Compare the letters of the words with their codes. Notice how the code letters are directly related in alphabetical order to the words. Find the new words by looking at the pattern and copying it.

22 **G B N F** To get from the word to the code, move each letter forwards one place.

23 **C B S O** To get from the word to the code, move each letter forwards one place.

24 **K N N J** To get from the word to the code, move each letter backwards one place.

25 **V H K C** To get from the word to the code, move each letter backwards one place.

26 **J C K T** To get from the word to the code, move each letter forwards two places.

27 **SOIL** To get from the code to the word, move each letter backwards one place.

28 **PORT** To get from the code to the word, move each letter backwards one place.

29 **FIRM** To get from the code to the word, move each letter forwards one place.

30 **CUBS** To get from the code to the word, move each letter backwards two places.

Focus test 8: Sequences
(pages 18–19)

1 **big, small** 'Big' and 'small' are antonyms in the same way as are 'high' and 'low'.

2 **paw, horse** A 'dog's' foot is a 'paw' in the same way as a 'horse's' foot is a 'hoof'.

3 **mouth, ears** You 'smile' with your 'mouth' in the same way as you 'listen' with your 'ears'.

4 **Bed, pillow** A 'pillow' can be found on a 'bed' in the same way as a 'cushion' is found on a 'chair'.

5 **hat, foot** A 'hat' fits onto a 'head' and a 'sock' fits onto a 'foot'.

6 **Hard, wide** 'Hard' and 'difficult' are synonyms in the same way as are 'wide' and 'broad'.

7 **WX** Each letter in the first pair moves forwards two places in the next pair.

8 **MN** This is a consecutive pattern following alphabetical order.

9 **RT** Each letter in the first pair moves forwards four places in the next pair.

10 **GH** Each letter in the first pair moves forwards one place in the next pair.

11 **TS** Each letter in the first pair moves backwards two places in the next pair.

12 **JJ** Each letter in the first pair moves forwards three places in the next pair.

13 **IJ, KL** This is a consecutive pattern following alphabetical order.

14 **Xw, Rq** This is a consecutive pattern following reverse alphabetical order; the first letter in each pair is upper case and the second is lower case.

15 **AC, QS** Each letter in the first pair moves forwards four places in the next pair.

16 **YI, XJ** The first letters are in an alternating pattern: XYXYXY. The second letter in each pair moves forwards one place.

17 **CJ, DK** Each letter moves forwards one place in the next pair.

18 **JF, MC** The first letters are in alphabetical order. The second letters are in reverse alphabetical order.

19 **XF, UL** The first letters are in reverse alphabetical order. The second letter in each pair moves forwards two places.

20 **Pq7, Rs8** Each letter moves forwards one place in the next trio. The first letter is upper case and the second lower case. The numbers increase by 1 each time.

21 **YZ, AB** This is a consecutive pattern following alphabetical order. When the end of the alphabet is reached, start afresh with A.

22 **ED, AZ** This is a consecutive pattern following reverse alphabetical order. When the beginning of the alphabet is reached, start afresh with Z.

23 **YB, SC** The first letters are in an alternating pattern: YSYSYS. The second letters are in alphabetical order.

24 **18, 9** The numbers decrease by 3 each time.

25 **7, 17** The numbers increase by 10 each time.

26 **9, 17** The numbers increase by 4 each time.

27 **25, 15** The numbers decrease by 10 each time.

28 **4, 16** This is a doubling pattern: the numbers are multiplied by 2 each time.

29 **66, 5** This is an alternating pattern. The first, third, fifth numbers are all 66. The second, fourth and sixth numbers increase by 1 each time.

30 **13, 18** The number added increases by 1 each time: +1, +2, +3, +4, +5.

Mixed paper 1: (pages 20–23)

1 **flat, level** Both words mean even.

2 **mutter, mumble** Both words mean to speak unclearly.

3 **shiny, bright** Both words mean sparkly and glossy.

4 **distant, far** Both words mean a long way away.

5 **wind, twist** Both words mean to turn or spiral.

6 **links**　　　　7 **berry**

8 **scour**　　　　9 **drums**

10 **spice**

11–15 **A: horse, rabbit, wolf, cheetah** All these are animals.

　　　B: rubber, pencil, sharpener All these are items of stationery.

　　　C: kitchen, bathroom, bedroom All these are rooms that can be found in a house.

16 <u>**clouds**</u>, **snow** During the night, snow fell and our garden was white.

17 <u>**box**</u>, **bottle** At the restaurant, the waiter opened a bottle of wine with the corkscrew.

18 <u>**cat**</u>, **dog** Sam gave his dog a bone after taking him for a walk in the park.

19 <u>**television**</u>, **telephone** The telephone rang and my mother answered it.

20 <u>**gnome**</u>, **bird** A robin is a garden bird with a red breast.

21 **t** biscuit, term　　22 **y** donkey, yard

23 **d** land, dragon　　24 **e** pile, enough

25 **f** cliff, forest

26–30 Three of the words begin with 'F', so 'F' = 8 and 'O' = 6. From this information, you can work out all the codes.

26 **FOOL** 8 = F, 6 = O, 6 = O, 9 = L

27 **OPEN** 6 = O, 7 = P, 4 = E, 3 = N

28 **FLAN** 8 = F, 9 = L, 1 = A, 3 = N

29 **FLAP** 8 = F, 9 = L, 1 = A, 7 = P

30 **PANE** 7 = P, 1 = A, 3 = N, 4 = E

31 **BUT** buttons　　32 **NEW** newspapers

33 **MEN** pavements　34 **AND** Scotland

35 **LAW** lawn　　　　36 **PLUMP**

37 **CHAIR**　　　　38 **STRUCK**

39 **START**　　　　40 **CLEVER**

41 **inflexible, pliable** 'Inflexible' means it cannot be bent whereas 'pliable' means its shape can be altered.

42 **combine, separate** To 'combine' means to join together whereas to 'separate' is to part.

43 **hurtle, plod** To 'hurtle' is to rush or move quickly whereas 'plod' means to move slowly and deliberately.

44 **craven, bold** 'Craven' means cowardly whereas 'bold' is brave.

45 **optimistic, downbeat** If you are 'optimistic', you are upbeat and positive whereas if you are 'downbeat', you are disheartened and sad.

46 **abundant, placid** The other words mean small in quantity.

47 **truthful, penitent** The other words mean respectful, loyal or submissive.

48 **shove, push** The other words are all associated with 'pulling' an object towards you. In 'push' and 'shove' the object goes away from you.

49 **poach, peril** The other words mean to mix something together or to disorganise.

50 **taut, negligent** The other words mean loose or floppy.

51 **d** 10 − (5 + 3) = 2

52 **e** 5 + 3 + 2 = 10

53 **e** 5 × 2 = 10

54 **b** 10 ÷ 2 = 5

55 **c** (10 − 3) − (3 + 1) = 3

56 **response, solution** A 'response' answers a 'query' in the same way as a 'solution' solves a 'problem'.

57 **outline, predicament** A 'silhouette' is similar to an 'outline' in the same way as a 'crisis' is similar to a disaster, difficulty or 'predicament'.

58 **lukewarm, apathetic** 'Lukewarm' and 'tepid' are synonyms in the same way as are 'half-hearted' and 'apathetic'.

59 **toe, wrist** A 'finger' and a 'toe' are the extremities of a body. The 'ankle' and 'wrist' are corresponding joints connecting the foot and hand to the limb.

60 **accept, respect** 'Decline' means to refuse and 'accept' is the opposite. To 'despise' is to hold in contempt and the opposite is to 'respect' or revere.

61 **breakage**　　62 **available**

63 **lighthouse**　64 **highlights**

65 **tenor**

Mixed paper 2: (pages 24–28)

1

D	R	E	A	M
	O		L	
G	A	M	E	S
	S		R	
S	T	A	T	E

2

B	R	A	I	N
	E		N	
S	P	I	N	E
	E		E	
F	L	A	R	E

3 **hat** The pattern is to change the middle letter from 'i' to 'a'.

4 **cook** The pattern is to keep the first letter of the first word and add the ending '-ook'.

5 **bus** The pattern is to keep the first three letters of the first word and delete the rest.

6 **LEAP**   **7** **EARTH**   **8** **RICH**

9 **COPY**   **10** **BEFORE**

11–15 Try each of the words in the first set of brackets. Do they make sense with any words in the second and third set of brackets? Only one combination of three words makes sense.

11 **sausages, chips, beans**

12 **Two, three, five**

13 **book, pages, exciting**

14 **birds, garden, feeding**

15 **bins, playground, school**

16 **k** crack, king; stock, kipper

17 **b** bob, berry; crab, box

18 **w** straw, wet; willow, want

19 **t** basket, top; knit, terror

20 **l** hail, let; call, lemon

21–23 Use a grid to help you.

B	L	U	E		1st
G	R	E	E	N	2nd
G	R	E	Y		3rd
R	E	D			4th
Y	E	L	L	O	W	5th

21 **GREEN**   **22** **GREY**   **23** **RED**

24 **A** You must use only the information you are given. B, C and D may or may not be true. Only 'All beetles are insects' must be true in this case.

25 **D** You must use only the information you are given. A, B and C may or may not be true. Only 'Some boys are called James' must be true in this case.

26 **PEAR** □ = P, △ = E, ÷ = A, ◊ = R

27 **TRAP** • = T, ◊ = R, ÷ = A, □ = P

28 **STAR** △ = S, • = T, ÷ = A, ◊ = R

29 **NEST** ○ = N, △ = E, △ = S, • = T

30 **TREE** • = T, ◊ = R, △ = E, △ = E

31 **up** upstairs, upstream, uphill, upon

32 **over** overhear, overgrown, overboard, overnight

33 **black** blackberry, blackboard, blackbird, blackcurrant

34 **snow** snowball, snowdrop, snowflake, snowplough

35 **water** waterfall, watercolour, waterski, waterproof

36 **b** rain, bramble   **37** **g** love, gate

38 **t** here, stick   **39** **r** gown, frill

40 **r** tickle, sport

41 **9, 7** The numbers decrease by 2 each time.

42 **5, 25** The numbers increase by 5 each time.

43 **15, 3** This is an alternating pattern. The first, third and fifth numbers increase by 1 each time. The second, fourth and sixth numbers are 15 each time.

44 **12, 22** The numbers increase by 10 each time.

45 **11, 16** The number added increases by 1 each time: +1, +2, +3, +4, +5.

46 **expose, conceal** 'Expose' means to show whereas 'conceal' means to hide.

47 **preference, indifference** 'Preference' means a greater liking of something whereas 'indifference' implies not taking an interest in something.

48 **abundant, scarce** 'Abundant' means there is a lot of something whereas 'scarce' means rare.

49 **gratified, displeased** 'Gratified' means you are pleased with something whereas 'displeased' means you are dissatisfied.

50 **soar, plummet** 'Soar' means to rise through the air whereas 'plummet' is to fall quickly down.

51 It was **raining** so hard this **morning**, we got soaked.

52 Our **dog** chewed my favourite teddy **bear**.

53 That vase of **flowers** on the **table** is pretty.

54 The old man drove his **car** carefully into the **garage**.

55 A fluffy, white **cloud** blew across the blue **sky**.

56 **amusing** Both words mean comical or humorous.

57 **tentative** Both words mean cautious or uncertain.

58 **composed** Both words mean cool-headed, serene, relaxed.

59 **frenetic** Both words mean panic-stricken or agitated.

60 **abysmal** Both words mean terrible or atrocious.

61 **FOIL**   **62** **TAME**

63 **WASH**   **64** **CITY**

65 **FIRM**

Mixed paper 3: (pages 28–32)

1 **LASS** 3 = L, 8 = A, 1 = S, 1 = S

2 **BEST** 4 = B, 2 = E, 1 = S, 5 = T

3 **5832** T = 5, A = 8, L = 3, E = 2

4 **2815** E = 2, A = 8, S = 1, T = 5

5 **LABEL** 3 = L, 8 = A, 4 = B, 2 = E, 3 = L

6 **stamp** 'Stamp' means to make something 'flat'

by 'pressing' on it; it can also mean to make a 'mark' by 'printing' on something.

7 **wing** A 'wing' can mean part of a large building as well as a bird's limb.

8 **iron** 'Iron' is a type of metal as well as an aid used to press one's clothes.

9 **star** A 'star' is a bright, twinkly object out in space as well as a famous person.

10 **over** 'Over' is a preposition meaning above the top of something as well as meaning something is completed.

11 **exceptional, ordinary** 'Exceptional' means outstanding whereas 'ordinary' means unremarkable.

12 **tardy, punctual** 'Tardy' means to be late whereas 'punctual' is to be on time.

13 **capable, inept** 'Capable' means skilful whereas 'inept' means incapable.

14 **modest, boastful** 'Modest' means humble or discreet whereas 'boastful' means arrogant or big-headed.

15 **entice, repel** 'Entice' means to attract whereas 'repel' means to disgust or put off.

16 **h** heat, hotter, hill, hanger

17 **r** rice, rant, reach, rafter

18 **t** tangle, that, teach, true

19 **b** bend, black, bother, band

20 **s** spear, smug, snow, soften

21 **PR** Each letter in the first pair moves forwards four places in the second pair.

22 **OW** The first letter moves backwards one place. The second letter moves forwards one place.

23 **WX** This is a consecutive pattern in alphabetical order.

24 **PU** Each letter in the first pair moves forwards one place in the second pair.

25 **DW** The first letter moves forwards one place. The second letter moves backwards one place.

26–30 Tommy is either in stable 5, 6 or 8. Crystal must therefore be 2 or 3. If Captain and Secret are next door and Secret has an end stable, Secret must be 5, Captain 6 and Tommy 8. If Paloma and Shadow are not next door to each other, Paloma must be 2 and Crystal 3.

26 **8**   27 **3**   28 **6**   29 **5**   30 **2**

31 **bean** He wants to **be an** astronaut when he grows up.

32 **slit** Fireworks **lit** up the dark night sky.

33 **tall** She blew out **all** the candles on her cake.

34 **they** My bicycle is chained to **the y**ard railings.

35 **verb** The ri**ver b**urst the far bank, flooding the valley.

36 **CHEAP**   37 **STEAM**
38 **CRATE**   39 **TEACH**
40 **CHARM**   41 **PAST**
42 **DEAD**   43 **CLAP**

44 **EVER**   45 **FOND**

46 **caught**, **fell** Sol slipped on the step and fell down onto the hard ground.

47 **presents**, **medals** At the Olympics, our country won lots of gold medals.

48 **table**, **egg** After clucking loudly, the hen laid a large egg in her nest box.

49 **mats**, **seats** The film had already started as we found our seats in the cinema.

50 **curtains**, **flowers** He walked into the garden and picked some pretty flowers.

51 **reduce** Both words mean to become smaller or diminish.

52 **grumble** Both words mean to complain or moan.

53 **stockpile** Both words mean a store of money or valuable objects.

54 **gangling** Both words mean ungracefully tall and thin.

55 **complex** Both words mean complicated.

56 **four, hours**

57 **close, behind**

58 **threw, board**

59 **mouse, floor**

60 **copied, written**

61 **antagonist, opponent** Both words mean an enemy or rival.

62 **moist, damp** Both words mean slightly wet.

63 **frustrate, thwart** Both words mean to impede, hinder or prevent.

64 **intrigue, absorb** Both words mean to fascinate, attract or interest.

65 **charm, allure** Both words mean fascination, attraction or appeal.

Mixed paper 4: (pages 33–36)

1 **15** $5 + 3 + 1 + 6 = 15$
2 **12** $6 + 3 + 1 + 2 = 12$
3 **10** $1 + 2 + 2 + 5 = 10$
4 **13** $1 + 3 + 3 + 6 = 13$
5 **16** $3 + 5 + 5 + 2 + 1 = 16$
6 **gain**   7 **roped**
8 **tread**   9 **toils**
10 **panic**
11 **RATES, STARE**
12 **SCALP, CLASP**
13 **GREAT, GRATE**
14 **FRAIL, FLAIR**
15 **STRAP, PARTS**
16 **barter, haggle** Both words mean to negotiate or to bargain.
17 **contrive, arrange** Both words mean to plot and plan.
18 **frustrate, thwart** Both words mean to hinder or impede.
19 **arctic, wintry** Both words mean freezing or

very cold.

20 **adjacent, bordering** Both words mean neighbouring or nearby.

21–25 Use grids as shown below to help work out the missing word.

21 **BEST**

		1	2		3	4	
P	O	U	R		G	E	T	S

		1	2		3	4	
R	O	B	E		S	T	E	P

22 **MIST**

		3	4		1	2	
C	A	M	E		S	O	F	A

		3	4		1	2	
P	O	S	T		M	I	L	K

23 **PILL**

	2	3	4?		4?			1
B	A	R	D		D	O	Z	Y

	2	3	4?		4?			1
S	I	L	T		L	O	O	P

24 **WANT**

1	2	3					4	
H	E	L	P		P	U	M	A

1	2	3					4	
W	A	N	D		C	I	T	Y

25 **STOP**

			4		1	3?	3?	2
C	R	E	W		F	O	O	L

			4		1	3?	3?	2
S	T	E	P		S	L	O	T

26–30 Try each of the words in the first set of brackets. Do they make sense with any words in the second and third set of brackets? Only one combination of three words makes sense.

26 **late, music, school**
27 **dog, wall, sister**
28 **athlete, receive, medal**
29 **frogs, caterpillars, butterflies**
30 **football, park, weekends**
31 **n** yawn, nothing
32 **r** flower, rush
33 **y** stay, yacht
34 **e** spike, entry
35 **h** rash, honey

36–40 Two words begin with S, so S = ①. SEEN can easily be identified as ① ⑥ ⑥ ③. From this, you can identify all the codes.

36 SEEN ① = S, ⑥ = E, ⑥ = E, ③ = N
37 NOSE ③ = N, ④ = O, ① = S, ⑥ = E
38 SANE ① = S, ⑤ = A, ③ = N, ⑥ = E
39 MOAN ② = M, ④ = O, ⑤ = A, ③ = N
40 ① ⑤ ② ⑥ S = ①, A = ⑤, M = ②, E = ⑥
41 **UA, RB** The first letters are in reverse alphabetical order. The second letters are in a repeating pattern: ABABAB.

42 **A3, b4** The letters are in alphabetical order but are alternating between capitals and lower case. The numbers are in a repeating pattern: 343434.

43 **JQ, LO** The first letters are in alphabetical order. The second letters are in reverse alphabetical order.

44 **AC, MO** Each letter moves forwards by four letters.

45 **XW, PO** This is a consecutive pattern in reverse alphabetical order.

46 STAIR
47 BATHE
48 STICK
49 FLOUR
50 SCARCE
51 LOW pillow
52 OWN down
53 NET nettles
54 SEA seaside
55 BAT bath
56 QUIRKY
57 SEIZE
58 ENTIRE
59 SERENE
60 SMUG
61 **cement** 'Separate' means to part whereas 'cement' is to join together or reinforce.
62 **vanquish** 'Lose' means to fail whereas 'vanquish' is to overcome, be successful.
63 **ecstasy** 'Agony' is severe pain whereas 'ecstasy' is complete elation or extreme joy.
64 **complete** 'Partial' is fractional whereas 'complete' is entire or whole.
65 **assist** 'Obstruct' is to get in the way of or hinder whereas 'assist' means to help or aid.

Mixed paper 5: (pages 36–40)

1 **13312** T = 1, O = 3, O = 3, T = 1, H = 2
2 **£ + ^ = M** = £, I = +, C = ^, E = =
3 **n k y u** B = n, O = k, T = y, H = u
4 **TREE** y = T, g = R, s = E, s = E
5 **O P U** Look at the relationship between the letters and the codes. Y = Z, E = F and S = T. To get from the word to the code, move each letter forwards one place. So, N = O, O = P, T = U.
6 DOCK   **7** SEEM   **8** DEAR
9 COLD   **10** SITE
11 **p** pear, peach, pink, particle
12 **f** flight, flower, fair, fill
13 **a** ago, amble, afloat, across
14 **m** mutter, mass, moral, mothers
15 **d** dairy, down, ditch, devil
16 **t** 5 + 3 + 4 = 12, 12 = t
17 **p** 12 − (2 × 5) = 2, 2 = p
18 **q** (12 − 3) − 4 = 5, 5 = q
19 **u** (10 ÷ 5) × 2 = 4, 4 = u
20 **s** (2 × 4) + (5 − 3) = 10, 10 = s
21 **insolent, impertinent** Both words mean rude or impudent.
22 **sifted, filtered** Both words mean strained or separated.

23 **dazzling**, **vivid** Both words mean brilliant or bright.

24 **concoction, mixture** Both words mean a brew or a potion.

25 **scurry, scuttle** Both words mean to scamper or dash.

26 **artistic** Both words mean imaginative or inventive.

27 **devious** Both words mean deceitful.

28 **impede** Both words mean to prevent.

29 **authentic** Both 'genuine' and 'authentic' mean something that is the real thing, not a fake.

30 **insincere** Both words mean lying or fraudulent.

31 **fur** A 'rabbit' may have all these things but 'fur' on its body is part of its being.

32 **nib** If a 'pen' does not have a 'nib' then it cannot write which is its purpose.

33 **a player** Of all these things 'a player' is essential.

34 **petals** 'Petals' are the only integral part of a 'rose' that is mentioned.

35 **stuffing** If a 'pillow' does not have 'stuffing' it cannot act like a cushion.

36 **north**   37 **east**

38 **south-east**   39 **shops**

40 **post office**

41–45 Two of the words start with B, so B = t. NEED must be j v v x because of the double E. From this information you can work out all the letters.

41 **BORN** t = B, u = O, s = R, j = N

42 **NEED** j = N, v = E, v = E, x = D

43 **BARN** t = B, k = A, s = R, j = N

44 **DARN** x = D, k = A, s = R, j = N

45 **s u x v** R = s, O = u, D = x, E = v

46 **love** lovesick, lovebird, loveable, loveless

47 **master** mastermind, masterpiece, masterclass, masterfully

48 **green** greenhouse, greengrocer, greenfly, greenfield

49 **grand** grandfather, grandparent, grandson, grandchild

50 **care** caretaker, careworn, carefree, careless

51 **gather** 'Strew' means to spread about whereas 'gather' is to collect or take in.

52 **ordinary** 'Bizarre' means peculiar whereas 'ordinary' means normal.

53 **undermine** 'Bolster' means to support or to build up whereas 'undermine' means to weaken or destabilise.

54 **enemy** 'Crony' means a friend or companion whereas 'enemy' means someone you are against or opposed to.

55 **few** 'Myriad' means a vast number whereas 'few' means a small number.

56 The kettle boiled and **Maria** made **herself** a cup of tea.

57 The carpenter **mended** the **broken** door.

58 We checked **in** four suitcases **at** the airport.

59 Would you like salad **or** vegetables **with** your steak?

60 The policeman **stopped** the man who was **driving** too fast.

61 **XY** The first letter in each pair moves forwards one place. The second letter moves backwards one place.

62 **OP** Each letter moves forwards four places.

63 **ZA** Each letter moves forwards two places. (When you reach the end of the alphabet wrap around to the beginning again: XYZABC.)

64 **NQ** Each letter moves forwards four places.

65 **OR** The first letter in each pair moves backwards one place. The second letter moves forwards one place.

Mixed paper 6: (pages 40–44)

1 **church, square**   2 **garden, across**

3 **stormy, waves**   4 **drink, snack**

5 **clock, three**

6 **8, 16** The numbers increase by 4 each time.

7 **26, 16** The numbers decrease by 5 each time.

8 **5, 33** This is an alternating pattern. The first, third and fifth number is 33. The second, fourth and sixth number increases by 1 each time.

9 **6, 5** This number subtracted decreases by 1 each time: −5, −4, −3, −2, −1.

10 **16a, 10d** The numbers decrease by 2 each time. The letters are in alphabetical order.

11 **CROOK**   12 **KNOT**

13 **NEST**   14 **SINGE**

15 **WEARY**

16–18 First put all the letters of CRADLE into alphabetical order: A C D E L R.

16 **A**   17 **R**   18 **D**

19 **four, Monday** Both come before the word in the sentence.

20 **hop, fly** Both refer to how the animal in the sentence moves.

21 **WORTH, THROW**

22 **THESE, SHEET**

23 **WORSE, SWORE**

24 **SPORT, PORTS**

25 **THORN, NORTH**

26 **evident, obscure** 'Evident' means obvious whereas 'obscure' means not clear.

27 **opaque, transparent** 'Opaque' means blocking the light whereas 'transparent' is see-through.

28 **congested, deserted** 'Congested' is very crowded whereas 'deserted' is empty.

29 **damage, enhance** To 'damage' is to spoil something whereas to 'enhance' something is

Bond Verbal Reasoning Assessment Papers Challenge 9–10 years

to improve it.

30 **obey, defy** To 'obey' is to do as you are told whereas to 'defy' is to go against someone's wishes.

31 **them** We scored four goals in **the m**atch.

32 **seat** The lighthouse warned ships on the **sea t**hat there were rocks nearby.

33 **then** In winter, the days are short and **the n**ights are long.

34 **tour** Please collec**t our** tickets from the desk.

35 **hear** The tourists walked slowly through t**he ar**ch.

36 **vibrate** Both words mean to tremble or shake quickly.

37 **isolation** Both words mean being on one's own.

38 **strenuous** Both words mean very tiring and demanding.

39 **stilted** Both words mean when a person is stiff and self-conscious in their manner.

40 **horrify** Both words mean to shock or dismay.

41 **green** A 'green' is a piece of open land for everyone to use, as well as a colour.

42 **box** A 'box' is a case or carton as well as a verb meaning to thump or clout.

43 **close** Close means nearby as well as describing when the air is humid.

44 **better** 'Better' means preferable as well as stronger and fitter (after an illness).

45 **under** 'Under' means subordinate as well as a preposition meaning the opposite of above.

46 **SANK** 3 = S, 7 = A, 1 = N, 0 = K

47 **3 5 7 6** S = 3, L = 5, A =7, B = 6

48 **BASE** 6 = B, 7 = A, 3 = S, 2 = E

49 **5 7 3 4** L = 5, A = 7, S = 3, T = 4

50 **TAKE** 4 = T, 7 = A, 0 = K, 2 = E

51 **hall** The pattern is to use the first two letters of the first word and add '-ll'.

52 **ride** The pattern is to reverse the first and the third letters of the first word. The other letters remain the same.

53 **are** The pattern is to use the second, third and fourth letters of the first word, in reverse order.

54 **paws** The pattern is to reverse the letters in the first word.

55 **sodden** The pattern is to reverse the first three letters of the first word, then add '-den'.

56–60 Use a grid to help you.

	cats	dogs	rabbits	budgies	chickens	guinea pigs
A	✓		✓			
B	✓	✓		✓		
C	✓				✓	
D		✓				✓
E		✓				
F			✓			

56 **B**   57 **E and F**   58 **D**

59 **4**   60 **B**

61 **F Y P B** To get from the word to the code, move each letter backwards two places. (When you reach the beginning of the alphabet, wrap around to the end of the alphabet, so CBAZYX.)

62 **EASY** To get from the code to the word, move each letter forwards two places.

63 **M B U F** To get from the word to the code, move each letter forwards one place.

64 **U J N F** To get from the word to the code, move each letter forwards one place.

65 **HOUR** To get from the code to the word, move each letter backwards one place.

Mixed paper 7: (pages 44–48)

1–5 Use grids as shown below to help work out the missing word.

1 **BIRD**

1	2	3			4			
H	A	R	K		P	I	N	G

1	2	3			4			
B	I	R	O		D	A	M	P

2 **HURT**

1	2						3/4	3/4
K	I	N	G		F	U	S	S

1	2						3/4	3/4
H	U	N	G		S	O	R	T

3 **SIDE**

1	4?		4?		3		2	
H	E	R	E		P	R	O	W

1	4?		4?		3		2	
S	O	M	E		D	R	I	P

4 **GATE**

			1			2	3	4
P	I	E	S		R	O	C	K

			1			2	3	4
F	R	O	G		L	A	T	E

5 **SPUR**

2		1/4			3			1/4
D	I	E	S		G	O	N	E

2		1/4			3			1/4
P	E	R	T		U	R	N	S

6 **silhouette, footpath** The other words mean to track or keep an eye on.

7 **conversational, plural** The other words mean extraordinary.

8 **gate, garden** The other words are all plants.

9 **bridge, road** The other words are bodies of water.

A10

10 **body, arm** The other words are at the extremity of a limb.

11 **14** 4 + 3 + 2 + 1 + 4 = 14

12 **22** 7 + 4 + 1 + 5 + 5 = 22

13 **19** 5 + 2 + 1 + 7 + 4 = 19

14 **B** You must use only the information given. A, C, D may or may not be true. Only 'People laugh at clowns in circuses' must be true in this case.

15 **C** You must use only the information given. A, B, D may or may not be true and, in this case, unlikely. Only 'It can rain on Fridays' must be true in this case.

16 **saturated, parched** 'Drenched' and 'saturated' are synonyms meaning very wet whereas 'arid' and 'parched' are synonyms meaning very dry.

17 **dated, contemporary** 'Dated' is the reverse of 'current' in the same way as 'contemporary' is the reverse of 'historical'.

18 **yell, debate** To 'bellow' and 'yell' are synonyms (meaning to shout), as are 'discuss' and 'debate' (meaning to talk through something or share different ideas).

19 **Tennis, racquet** You play 'tennis' with a 'racquet' in the same way that you play 'cricket' with a 'bat'.

20 **road, train** A 'car' travels on a 'road' in the same way that a 'train' travels on 'tracks'.

21–25 The milk is on the bottom row under the fruit juice so, milk = G and fruit juice C. The British cheese is next to the French cheese so it must be A. Therefore, fresh pastry = D. This leaves cream = F.

21 **A**   22 **G**   23 **D**   24 **C**   25 **F**

26 **CD, LM** Each letter moves forwards three places.

27 **FH, NP** Each letter moves forwards four places.

28 **BM, FQ** Each letter moves forwards two places.

29 **SF, UD** The first letter moves forwards in alphabetical order. The second letter moves in reverse alphabetical order.

30 **BC, DB** The first letter in each pair moves forwards two places. The second letters are in an alternating pattern: CBCBCB.

31 **agree** 'Consent' and 'agree' mean to allow or assent.

32 **redden** 'Blush' and 'redden' mean to colour up in the face.

33 **achieve** 'Attain' and 'achieve' mean to succeed.

34 **wince** 'Cringe' and 'wince' mean to squirm or recoil or flinch.

35 **tremble** 'Quake' and 'tremble' mean to shake.

36 **they** The hawk killed **the y**oung bird in my garden.

37 **vest** Our class bookshel**ves t**umbled down, making us jump.

38 **love** My broken glass shattered al**l over** the floor.

39 **herd** **Her d**onkey has a loud bray and huge ears!

40 **vein** Polar bears survi**ve in** very cold conditions.

41 **skimpy, meagre** Both words mean insufficient.

42 **loyal, steadfast** Both words mean trusty or true.

43 **malice, spite** Both words mean ill will or hostility.

44 **earnest, sincere** Both words mean intense and serious.

45 **carcass, corpse** Both words mean a dead body.

46 **postman**   47 **starlight**

48 **below**   49 **shipwreck**

50 **ballroom**

51 **p** stamp, pick; stop, pea

52 **r** bar, rash; purr, ration

53 **e** purse, end; cure, eat

54 **g** gang, grow; spring, grab

55 **h** high, hoe; with, help

56 **# & * ^** G = #, R = &, I = *, P = ^

57 **NIPS** + = N, * = I, ^ = P, $ = S

58 **@ g 8 4** T = @, W = g, I = 8, N = 4

59 **RENT** D = R, > = E, 4 = N, @ = T

60 **U Y C P** To get from the word to the code, move each letter forwards two places.

61 **DUSK**   62 **COME**

63 **PONY**   64 **TOLL**

65 **VAIN**

Mixed paper 8: (pages 49–52)

1 **treat** There is only one 't' in 'CENTRAL'.

2 **steer** There is only one 'e' in 'WINTERS'.

3 **spies** There is only one 's' in 'MAGPIES'.

4 **rears** There is only one 'r' in 'SPEAKER'.

5 **sneer** There is only one 'e' in 'FINGERS'.

6 **n** sack, lawn   7 **k** nave, knit

8 **g** reed, grasp   9 **a** bred, spray

10 **c** sale, scour

11 **calf, foal** because both are the names for the young animal in the sentence.

12 **rude, trustworthy** because both are synonyms for the preceding word in the sentence; 'insolent' and 'rude' are similar and 'honest' and 'trustworthy' are similar.

13–15 Write out the letters of KETTLES in alphabetical order: EEKLSTT.

13 **T**   14 **E**   15 **L**

16 **hall** He was delighted wit**h all** his presents.

Bond Verbal Reasoning Assessment Papers Challenge 9–10 years

17 **move** It rained all day and the strea**m ov**erflowed.

18 **chin** Bats manage to cat**ch in**sects while they are flying.

19 **lord** We had to put words in alphabetica**l ord**er.

20 **wasp** Mac **was p**leased with his test result.

21 **C B M M** To get from the word to the code, move each letter forwards one place.

22 **R M L C** To get from the word to the code, move each letter backwards two places.

23 **FIRM** To get from the code to the word, move each letter forwards one place.

24 **STIR** To get from the code to the word, move each letter backwards one place.

25 **BEAK** To get from the code to the word, move each letter forwards three places. (When you reach the end of the alphabet, wrap around to start again: XYZABC.)

26 **b** (20 ÷ 5) × 3 = 12, 12 = b

27 **f** 2 + 5 + 1 + 12 = 20, 20 = f

28 **e** (5 × 3) − (1 × 12) = 3, 3 = e

29 **f** (12 ÷ 3) × 5 = 20, 20 = f

30 **c** (20 − 12) − (2 + 5) = 1, 1 = c

31–35 Use grids as shown below to help work out the missing word.

31 **ROSE**

3	2	1	4?
M	A	D	E

			4?
T	U	N	E

3	2	1	4?
S	O	R	T

			4?
J	A	D	E

32 **EXIT**

	2		1
Z	I	P	S

4	3?	3?	
E	D	D	Y

	2		1
A	X	L	E

4	3?	3?	
T	I	D	Y

33 **TEAM**

	3?	1	2
G	A	M	E

		3?	4
C	L	A	N

	3?	1	2
R	A	T	E

		3?	4
C	L	A	M

34 **GOLD**

	2/3	2/3	4
H	O	O	D

1			
F	L	I	P

	2/3	2/3	4
C	O	L	D

1			
G	R	E	W

35 **LOOP**

	2?	2?	1
Z	O	O	M

	3	4	
H	A	N	D

	2?	2?	1
P	O	O	L

	3	4	
R	O	P	E

36 **aggravate** 'Soothe' means to calm whereas 'aggravate' means agitate.

37 **elderly** 'Juvenile' means young whereas 'elderly' means old.

38 **bogus** 'Genuine' means real whereas 'bogus' means fake.

39 **persevere** 'Surrender' means to give in whereas 'persevere' means to continue to strive.

40 **obvious** 'Obscure' means not clear whereas 'obvious' means clear.

41 **HARE** 42 **BENT**

43 **BURY** 44 **WIND**

45 **COPE** 46 **STEAL**

47 **TOAST** 48 **TOWER**

49 **FREED** 50 **DANGER**

51–53 Suki is 3rd. If Sue, Corinne and Hamish are in a line, they must be in the last three places in the queue (4th, 5th and 6th), so Malek (who is at one end of the queue) must be 1st. Hamish and Bo have 3 people between them so Hamish must be 6th and Bo must be 2nd. Corinne is next to Hamish (5th) and Sue is next to her (4th).

51 **Bo** 52 **Hamish** 53 **Sue**

54–55 A table is the easiest way to sort the information, like this:

	curry	sausages	lasagne
A	✓		
B	✓		
C	✗	✓	
D		✓	✓
E		✓	

54 **sausages** 55 **D**

56 **tarnish, sully** Both words mean to spoil.

57 **thorough, rigorous** Both words mean doing something with great attention to detail.

58 **spout, spurt** Both words mean to gush or squirt.

59 **deflect, divert** Both words mean redirect or transfer.

60 **acidic, tart** Both words mean sharp or sour.

61 **BP, XM** The first letters are in an alternating pattern: BXBXBX. The second letters are in reverse alphabetical order.

62 **NL, QI** The first letters are in alphabetical order. The second letters are in reverse alphabetical order.

63 **OP, ST** This is a consecutive pattern in alphabetical order.

64 **Yb, Ve** The first letters are in reverse alphabetical order (capitals). The second letters are in alphabetical order (lower case).

65 **po, ON** There is an alternating pattern of lower case and capital letters. Both letters are in reverse alphabetical order.

A12

Give the missing two numbers in the following sequence.

Example 2   4   6   8   <u>10</u>   <u>12</u>

41 13   11   __   __   5   3

42 __   10   15   20   __   30

43 1   15   2   __   __   15

44 2   __   __   32   42   52

45 1   2   4   7   __   __

5

Underline the pair of words most opposite in meaning.

Example cup, mug   coffee, milk   <u>hot, cold</u>

46 stick, adhere   reveal, display   expose, conceal

47 preference, indifference   clamour, commotion   concern, worry

48 lie, fabrication   truth, veracity   abundant, scarce

49 contented, satisfied   thrilled, delighted   gratified, displeased

50 soar, plummet   extended, stretched   arise, ascend

5

Find and underline the two words that need to change places for each sentence to make sense.

Example She went to <u>letter</u> the <u>write</u>.

51 It was morning so hard this raining, we got soaked.

52 Our bear chewed my favourite teddy dog.

53 That vase of table on the flowers is pretty.

54 The elderly man drove his garage carefully into the car.

55 A fluffy, white sky blew across the blue cloud.

5

Work out the missing synonym. Spell the new word correctly, putting one letter in each space.

Example strange   p e __ __ l __ __ r   (peculiar)

56 droll   a m __ s __ __ __

57 unsure   t e n __ __ t i __ __

58 collected   c o m __ __ s __ __

59 hectic   f r __ n __ t __ __

60 dreadful   __ b __ __ __ a l

Change the first word into the last word by changing one letter at a time and making a new, different word in the middle.

Example   CASE   <u>CASH</u>   LASH

61   FAIL   _____   SOIL

62   CAME   _____   TALE

63   WASP   _____   MASH

64   PITY   _____   CITE

65   FILM   _____   FARM

Now go to the Progress Chart to record your score!   Total   65

Mixed paper 3

The code for STABLES is 1 5 8 4 3 2 1. Decode these into words.

1   3 8 1 1   _____   **2**   4 2 1 5   _____

Encode these words using the same code.

3   TALE   _____   **4**   EAST   _____

Using the same code, decode:

5   3 8 4 2 3.   _____

Underline the one word in the brackets that will go equally well with both pairs of words outside the brackets.

Example   rush, attack   cost, fee   (price, hasten, strike, <u>charge</u>, money)

6   flatten, press down   print, mark   (tread, parcel, letter, stamp, crush)

7   annexe, extension   fly, limb   (wing, house, feather, plane, arm)

8   metal, unbending   uncrease, straighten   (steel, lead, iron, smooth, heat)

9	planet, constellation	celebrity, personality	(moon, sun, star, galaxy, world)	
10	above, higher than	finished, ended	(on, excessive, dead, beyond, over)	5

Underline the two words, one from each group, that are most opposite in meaning.

Example (dawn, <u>early</u>, wake)   (<u>late</u>, stop, sunrise)

11	(essential, exceptional, misunderstood)	(ordinary, outstanding, gigantic)	
12	(tardy, miserly, forgetful)	(punctual, late, remiss)	
13	(changeable, capable, constant)	(skilful, inept, doubtful)	
14	(modest, arrogant, vain)	(modern, caring, boastful)	
15	(enlarge, engorge, entice)	(repel, attract, tempt)	5

Which one letter can be added to the front of all of these words to make new words?

Example __are   __at   __rate   __all   <u>c</u>

16	__eat	__otter	__ill	__anger	__	
17	__ice	__ant	__each	__after	__	
18	__angle	__hat	__each	__rue	__	
19	__end	__lack	__other	__and	__	
20	__pear	__mug	__now	__often	__	5

Fill in the missing letters. The alphabet has been written out to help you.

A B C D E F G H I J K L M N O P Q R S T U V W X Y Z

Example AB is to CD as PQ is to <u>RS</u>.

21 DF is to HJ as LN is to ___.

22 GM is to FN as PV is to ___.

23 QR is to ST as UV is to ___.

24 MR is to NS as OT is to ___.

25 AZ is to BY as CX is to ___.

(29)

At a riding stable, there are eight stables in two rows opposite each other. From the information, work out which horse is in each stable.

STABLE BLOCK A

1	2	3	4
BLACK BEAUTY			SHADOW

WALKWAY

5	6	7	8
		TRIGGER	

STABLE BLOCK B

Tommy is in the same row as Trigger but not the same as Crystal.

Captain is next to Secret in the same row. Secret has one of the end stables.

Paloma is unkind to Shadow. They are not in next-door stables.

26 Tommy is in stable number _____.

27 Crystal is in stable number _____.

28 Captain is in stable number _____.

29 Secret is in stable number _____.

30 Paloma is in stable number _____.

Find the four-letter word hidden at the end of one word and the beginning of the next word in each sentence. The order of the letters may not be changed.

Example   We had bat<u>s and</u> balls.   <u>sand</u>

31 He wants to be an astronaut when he grows up.   _____

32 Fireworks lit up the dark night sky.   _____

33 She blew out all the candles on her cake.   _____

34 My bicycle is chained to the yard railings.   _____

35 The river burst the far bank, flooding the valley.   _____

Rearrange the letters in capitals to make another word. The new word has something to do with the first two words or phrases.

Example spot   soil   SAINT   <u>STAIN</u>

36 low price   inexpensive   PEACH   _____

37 hot vapour   water droplets MEATS   _____

38 container   case   TRACE   _____

39 instruct   educate   CHEAT   _____

40 enchant   delight   MARCH   _____

5

Remove one letter from the word in capital letters to leave a new word. The meaning of the new word is given in the clue.

Example AUNT   an insect   <u>ANT</u>

41 PASTE   ended   _____

42 DREAD   not alive   _____

43 CLASP   applaud   _____

44 LEVER   always   _____

45 FOUND   keen on   _____

5

Change one word so that the sentence makes sense. Underline the word you are taking out and write your new word on the line.

Example   I waited in line to buy a <u>book</u> to see the film.   <u>ticket</u>

46 Sol slipped on the step and caught down onto the
    hard ground.   _____

47 At the Olympics, our country won lots of gold presents.   _____

48 After clucking loudly, the hen laid a large table in her
    nest box.   _____

49 The film had already started as we found our mats in
    the cinema.   _____

50 He walked into the garden and picked some pretty
    curtains.   _____

5

31

Work out the missing synonym. Spell the new word correctly, putting one letter in each space.

Example strange   p e __ __ l __ __ r   (peculiar)

51 taper   r __ d __ __ __

52 quibble   g r __ __ b __ __

53 hoard   s t __ __ k p i __ __

54 lanky   g a n g __ __ __ __

55 difficult   c o m __ __ __ __

5

Rearrange the muddled words in capital letters so that each sentence makes sense.

Example There are sixty SNODCES <u>seconds</u> in a UTMINE <u>minute</u>.

56 There are twenty-UROF _____ RSUHO _____ in a day.

57 Please SECOL _____ the door quietly HIBEDN _____ you.

58 The darts player WRETH _____ his dart accurately at the DROBA _____.

59 The little MSOUE _____ scampered across the ROLOF _____.

60 We PICODE _____ down what the teacher had WTTENRI _____.

5

Underline the pair of words most similar in meaning.

Example come, go   <u>roams, wanders</u>   fear, fare

61 antagonist, opponent   neighbour, friend   ally, competitor

62 simplify, complicate   apex, base   moist, damp

63 courage, compassion   frustrate, thwart   tardy, punctual

64 victorious, vigour   intrigue, absorb   absorb, exude

65 charismatic, unattractive   repulsion, fascination   charm, allure

5

If m = 6, r = 1, o = 3, e = 2 and f = 5, what are the totals of these words?

1 form _____

2 more _____

3 reef _____

4 room _____

5 offer _____

5

Underline the one word in each group that **can be made** from the letters of the word in capital letters.

Example	CHAMPION	camping	notch	peach	cramp	<u>chimp</u>
6	DANCING	grace	cling	gain	icing	grand
7	DROPPED	roped	prods	error	drops	pedal
8	TRACKED	crack	tread	rakes	darts	cakes
9	FLORIST	stiff	toils	forest	store	relief
10	CAMPING	cramp	image	grain	clamp	panic

5

Underline the two words that are made from the same letters.

Example	TAP	PET	<u>TEA</u>	POT	<u>EAT</u>
11	STRUT	RATES	STARE	STEER	RUSTY
12	PASTE	STRIP	SCARF	SCALP	CLASP
13	GRASP	GREAT	TRADE	GRATE	BUDGE
14	FIERY	FRAIL	FAIRY	RIFLE	FLAIR
15	STRAP	SPARE	PARTS	STAMP	PRISM

5

Underline the two words, one from each group, that are the closest in meaning.

Example (race, shop, <u>start</u>) (finish, <u>begin</u>, end)

16 (barter, buy, relinquish) (haggle, demonstrate, distribute)

17 (compare, contrive, conceive) (arrange, alter, assign)

18 (reassure, simplify, frustrate) (thwart, confuse, frighten)

19 (summer, seasonal, arctic) (artificial, wintry, weekly)

20 (adjacent, brimful, closefitting) (bordering, distant, perimeter)

5

Look at the first group of three words. The word in the middle has been made from the two other words. Complete the second group of three words in the same way, making a new word in the middle of the group.

Example PAIN INTO <u>TOOK</u>   ALSO <u>SOON</u> ONLY

21	POUR	URGE	GETS	ROBE	_____	STEP
22	CAME	SOME	SOFA	POST	_____	MILK
23	BARD	YARD	DOZY	SILT	_____	LOOP
24	HELP	HELM	PUMA	WAND	_____	CITY
25	CREW	FLOW	FOOL	STEP	_____	SLOT	5

Complete the following sentences by selecting the most sensible word from each group of words given in the brackets. Underline the words selected.

Example   The (<u>children</u>, boxes, foxes) carried the (houses, <u>books</u>, steps) home from the (greengrocer, <u>library</u>, factory).

26 On Tuesdays, I am (late, hungry, ill) home as I have a (custard, music, blue) lesson at (school, home, hospital).

27 That fierce (chicken, aeroplane, dog) barked at us over the garden (wall, window, doll) and frightened my little (sister, telephone, spider).

28 At the Olympics, the winning (athlete, boat, horse) climbed onto the podium to (receive, throw, lose) the gold (statue, ring, medal).

29 Tadpoles turn into (cats, frogs, beetles) and (piglets, puppies, caterpillars) turn into (geese, butterflies, chickens).

30 We like to kick a (wall, football, boot) about in the (car, park, traffic) at (weekends, first, them). 5

Find the letter that will end the first word and start the second word.

Example   drow (<u>n</u>) ought

31 yaw (__) othing   32 flowe (__) ush   33 sta (__) acht

34 spik (__) ntry   35 ras (__) oney   5

Match the correct code to each of the words below.

	MOAN	SANE	SEEN	NOSE
	❶❺❸❻	❷❹❺❸	❸❹❶❻	❶❻❻❸

36 ❶❻❻❸ _____   37 ❸❹❶❻ _____

38 ❶ ❺ ❸ ❻ _____   **39** ❷ ❹ ❺ ❸ _____

40 Using the same code, what is the code for SAME?   _____

5

Give the two missing pairs of letters and numbers in the following sequences. The alphabet has been written out for you.

A B C D E F G H I J K L M N O P Q R S T U V W X Y Z

Example	CQ	DP	EQ	FP	<u>GQ</u>	<u>HP</u>
41	WA	VB	__	TB	SA	__
42	__	__	C3	d4	E3	f4
43	HS	IR	__	KP	__	MN
44	__	EG	IK	__	QS	UW
45	ZY	__	VU	TS	RQ	__

5

Add one letter to the word in capital letters to make a new word. The meaning of the new word is given in the clue.

Example PLAN   simple   <u>PLAIN</u>

46	STAR	step	_____
47	BATH	to wash	_____
48	SICK	glue	_____
49	FOUR	ground grain	_____
50	SCARE	rare	_____

5

Find the three-letter word that can be added to the letters in capitals to make a new word. The new word will complete the sentence sensibly. Write the three-letter word.

Example The cat sprang onto the MO.   <u>USE</u>

51 At a sleepover, we had a PIL fight.   _____

52 We walked D the steep hill together.   _____

53 Our garden has lots of stinging TLES and other weeds.   _____

54 We made sandcastles on our day out at the SIDE.   _____

55 After the rugby match, Simon had a nice, hot H.   _____

5

Find a word that is similar in meaning to the word in capital letters and that rhymes with the second word.

Example	CABLE	tyre	<u>WIRE</u>
56	UNUSUAL	murky	_____
57	HIJACK	breeze	_____
58	WHOLE	wire	_____
59	CALM	marine	_____
60	COMPLACENT	plug	_____

5

Underline the one word in brackets that is most opposite in meaning to the word in capitals.

Example	WIDE	(broad	vague	long	<u>narrow</u>	motorway)
61	SEPARATE	(cement	clarify	organise	divide	divorce)
62	LOSE	(firm	confuse	vanquish	expel	battle)
63	AGONY	(depression	ecstasy	contentment	pain	soothing)
64	PARTIAL	(prejudiced	fractional	restricted	fond	complete)
65	OBSTRUCT	(teach	prohibit	assist	impede	construct)

5

Now go to the Progress Chart to record your score! Total 65

Mixed paper 5

1 If the code for SMOOTH is 5 4 3 3 1 2, what is the code for TOOTH? _____

2 If the code for CRIMES is ^ * + £ = @, what is the code for MICE? _____

3 If the code for BROTHER is n g k y u s g, what is the code for BOTH? _____

4 Using the same code, decode y g s s. _____

5 If the code for YES is Z F T, what is the code for NOT? _____

5

Change the first word into the last word by changing one letter at a time and making a new, different word in the middle.

Example <u>CASE</u>   <u>CASH</u>   LASH

6 LOCK   _____   DECK

7 SEAM   _____   SEEN

8 DEER   _____   DEAF

9 TOLD   _____   COLT

10 BITE   _____   SIZE

5

Which one letter can be added to the front of all of these words to make new words?

Example __are   __at   __rate   __all   <u>c</u>

11 __ear   __each   __ink   __article   ___

12 __light   __lower   __air   __ill   ___

13 __go   __mble   __float   __cross   ___

14 __utter   __ass   __oral   __others   ___

15 __airy   __own   __itch   __evil   ___

5

If $p = 2$, $q = 5$, $r = 3$, $s = 10$, $t = 12$ and $u = 4$, work out the answer to these. Write each answer as a letter.

16 $q + r + u =$ _____

17 $t - (pq) =$ _____

18 $(t - r) - u =$ _____

19 $(s \div q) \times p =$ _____

20 $(p \times u) + (q - r) =$ _____

5

Underline the pair of words most similar in meaning.

Example come, go   <u>roams, wanders</u>   fear, fare

21 insolent, impertinent   impudent, funny   cheeky, cheerful

22 scientific, natural   sifted, filtered   entirely, partially

23 brave, cowardly   dazzling, vivid   reasonable, appalling

24	concoction, mixture	destroy, fabricate	official, casual	

25	saunter, rush	fact, fiction	scurry, scuttle	5

Work out the missing synonym. Spell the new word correctly, putting one letter in each space.

Example strange   p e __ __ l __ __ r   (peculiar)

26 creative   a __ __ __ __ t i c

27 crafty   d e v __ __ __ __

28 block   i __ p __ __ __

29 genuine   a__t__e__ __ic

30 dishonest   i n s i n __ __ __ __   **5**

Choose the word or phrase that makes each sentence true.

Example   A LIBRARY always has (posters, a carpet, <u>books</u>, DVDs, stairs).

31 A RABBIT always has (a carrot, a hutch, fur, a warren, babies).

32 A PEN always has (paper, colours, a nib, writing, a cap).

33 A GAME always has (written rules, cheats, balls, captains, a player).

34 A ROSE always has (a smell, petals, sunshine, an arch, a red colour).

35 A PILLOW always has (a bed, stuffing, feathers, a pillowcase, a head).   **5**

Using the map below, select the correct compass points in the questions.

LIBRARY	POST OFFICE
AL'S HOUSE	
SHOPS	DOCTOR'S SURGERY

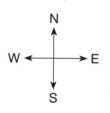

36 The library is due _____ from the shops.

37 The post office is due _____ from the library.

38 Which direction does Al go from his house to the doctors' surgery?   _____

39 What is south-west from Al's house?   _____

40 What is north-east from Al's house?   _____   **5**

Match the correct code to the words below.

	BARN	NEED	DARN	BORN

41 t u s j   ———

42 j v v x   ———

43 t k s j   ———

44 x k s j   ———

45 Using the same code, what is RODE?   ———

5

Find a word that can be put in front of each of the following words to make new, compound words.

Example	cast	fall	ward	pour	<u>down</u>
46	sick	bird	able	less	———
47	mind	piece	class	fully	———
48	house	grocer	fly	field	———
49	father	parent	son	child	———
50	taker	worn	free	less	———

5

Underline the one word in brackets that is most opposite in meaning to the word in capitals.

Example WIDE (broad   vague   long   <u>narrow</u>   motorway)

51 STREW (gather   distribute   scatter   clutter   sprinkle)

52 BIZARRE (purchase   trade   ordinary   weird   curious)

53 BOLSTER (strengthen   undermine   encourage   sustain   fortify)

54 CRONY (ally   comrade   conspirator   acquaintance   enemy)

55 MYRIAD (countless   few   numerous   innumerable   boundless)

5

Find and underline the two words that need to change places for each sentence to make sense.

Example She went to <u>letter</u> the <u>write</u>.

56 The kettle boiled and herself made Maria a cup of tea.

57 The carpenter broken the mended door.

58 We checked at four suitcases in the airport.

59 Would you like salad with vegetables or your steak?

60 The policeman driving the man who was stopped too fast.

5

Fill in the missing letters. The alphabet has been written out to help you.

A B C D E F G H I J K L M N O P Q R S T U V W X Y Z

Example   AB is to CD as PQ is to <u>RS</u>.

61 AD is to BC as WZ is to ___.   **62** CD is to GH as KL is to ___.

63 TU is to VW as XY is to ___.   **64** BE is to FI as JM is to ___.

65 HI is to GJ as PQ is to ___.

5

Now go to the Progress Chart to record your score!   Total   65

Mixed paper 6

Rearrange the muddled words in capital letters so that each sentence makes sense.

Example   There are sixty SNODCES <u>seconds</u> in a UTMINE <u>minute</u>.

1 The RCHUCH _____ bells rang out across the QSUREA _____.

2 I saw a fox in the DNEAGR _____ of a house SCROAS _____ the road.

3 It was YMORTS _____ when we crossed the sea and the VSEWA _____ were big.

4 We stopped for a RDNIK _____ and a SKNAC _____ halfway through our journey.

5 The grandfather CKOLC _____ chimed RETHE _____ times.

5

Give the two missing numbers and/or letters in the following sequences.

Example   2   4   6   8   <u>10</u>   <u>12</u>

6 4   __   12   __   20   24

7 36   31   __   21   __   11

8	33	—	33	6	—	7
9	20	15	11	8	—	—
10	—	14b	12c	—	8e	6f

5

Add one letter to the word in capital letters to make a new word. The meaning of the new word is given in the clue.

Example PLAN   simple   <u>PLAIN</u>

11   COOK   a shepherd's staff   _____

12   NOT   a fastening   _____

13   NET   for eggs   _____

14   SING   burn lightly   _____

15   WEAR   tired   _____

5

If the letters in the word CRADLE are put into alphabetical order:

16   which comes first?   _____

17   which comes last?   _____

18   which comes third?   _____

3

Find two words, one from each set in brackets, that will complete the sentence in the most sensible way. Underline both words.

Example   Flea is to (fly, <u>flee</u>, insect) as bear is to (fur, dog, <u>bare</u>).

19   Five is to (four, six, ten) as Tuesday is to (Friday, Monday, Thursday).

20   Rabbit is to (roll, slither, hop) as bee is to (buzz, fly, swim).

2

Underline the two words that are made from the same letters.

Example	TAP	PET	<u>TEA</u>	POT	<u>EAT</u>
21	THROB	WORTH	WAIST	THROW	STRAW
22	BIRTH	THESE	SHAME	MATHS	SHEET
23	ROAST	STORE	RESTS	WORSE	SWORE
24	POSTS	TRAPS	SPORT	SPURT	PORTS
25	SHINS	THORN	THINS	NORTH	HANDS

5

Underline the pair of words most opposite in meaning.

Example cup, mug coffee, milk <u>hot, cold</u>

26 numb, senseless untruth, falsehood evident, obscure

27 opaque, transparent clammy, soggy blunder, error

28 teeming, swarming congested, deserted dither, falter

29 damage, enhance mar, ruin impair, blight

30 object, protest complain, contain obey, defy ⬭ 5

Find the four-letter word hidden at the end of one word and the beginning of the next word in each sentence. The order of the letters may not be changed.

Example We had bat<u>s and</u> balls. *sand*

31 We scored four goals in the match. _____

32 The lighthouse warned ships on the sea that there were rocks nearby. _____

33 In winter, the days are short and the nights are long. _____

34 Please collect our tickets from the desk. _____

35 The tourists walked slowly through the arch. _____ ⬭ 5

Underline the word in brackets closest in meaning to the word in capitals.

Example UNHAPPY (unkind death laughter <u>sad</u> friendly)

36 QUIVER (sag breathe vibrate taunt comfort)

37 SOLITUDE (isolation attitude imprisonment interaction secret)

38 EXHAUSTING (active baleful determined exercise strenuous)

39 WOODEN (forest relaxed natural stilted leafless)

40 APPAL (attract horrify depressed astonish humiliate) ⬭ 5

Underline the one word in the brackets that will go equally well with both pairs of words outside the brackets.

Example rush, attack cost, fee (price, hasten, strike, <u>charge</u>, money)

41 common land, grassed area emerald, jade (field, olive, green, vegetation, park)

42 container, a confined space punch, hit (slap, pot, box, jar, bottle)

42

43 near, adjacent	muggy, humid	(stuffy, close, even, well-matched, airless)
44 more desirable, effective	recovered, well	(cured, solved, improve, better, nicer)
45 lower level, lower grade	below, beneath	(above, higher, inside, through, under)

If the code for BLANKETS is 6 5 7 1 0 2 4 3, work out the following.

46 Decode 3 7 1 0. _____

47 Encode SLAB. _____

48 Decode 6 7 3 2. _____

49 Encode LAST. _____

50 Decode 4 7 0 2. _____

Change the first word of the third pair in the same way as the other pairs to give a new word.

Example	bind, hind	bare, hare	but, <u>hut</u>
51	catch, call	batch, ball	hatch, _____
52	robe, bore	tale, late	dire, _____
53	fronds, nor	stamen, mat	berate, _____
54	mood, doom	drab, bard	swap, _____
55	duster, sudden	damply, madden	dosing _____

Six friends have pets. From the information below, answer the questions.

A, B and C have cats. B, D and E have dogs.

A and F have rabbits. B has budgies in the garden in an aviary.

C has chickens and D has guinea pigs.

56 Who has a cat as well as a dog? _____

57 Which children have only one type of pet? _____

58 Who has a dog and guinea pigs? _____

59 How many types of animals do C and D have between them? _____

60 Who has the most types of animals? _____ ⬤ 5

A B C D E F G H I J K L M N O P Q R S T U V W X Y Z

61 If the code for SIMPLE is Q G K N J C, what is the code for HARD? _____

62 Using the same code, decode C Y Q W. _____

If the code for EARLY is F B S M Z, what is the code for:

63 LATE? _____

64 TIME? _____

65 Using the same code, decode I P V S. _____ ⬤ 5

Now go to the Progress Chart to record your score! Total ⬤ 65

Mixed paper 7

Look at the first group of three words. The word in the middle has been made from the two other words. Complete the second group of three words in the same way, making a new word in the middle of the group.

Example	PA<u>IN</u>	INTO	<u>TOO</u>K	ALSO	<u>SOON</u>	ONLY
1	HARK	HARP	PING	BIRO	_____	DAMP
2	KING	KISS	FUSS	HUNG	_____	SORT
3	HERE	HOPE	PROW	SOME	_____	DRIP
4	PIES	SOCK	ROCK	FROG	_____	LATE
5	DIES	EDGE	GONE	PERT	_____	URNS

⬤ 5

Underline the two words that are the odd ones out in the following group of words.

Example	black	<u>king</u>	purple	green	<u>house</u>
6	follow	shadow	silhouette	trail	footpath
7	remarkable	conversational	astonishing	plural	exceptional

44

8 gate	tree	flower	garden	weed
9 river	bridge	stream	canal	road
10 paw	hoof	body	foot	arm

⬭ 5

If e = 2, a = 1, s = 7, t = 4, f = 5 and r = 3, what are the totals of these words?

11 treat _____ 12 staff _____ 13 feast _____

⬭ 3

Read the first two statements and then underline one of the four options below that must be true.

14 Clowns often perform in circuses. Clowns make people laugh.

A Circuses tour the country. B People laugh at clowns in circuses.

C People don't cry at circuses. D Clowns are only found in circuses.

15 Today is Friday. It is rainy today.

A It always rains on Fridays. B It only rains on Fridays.

C It can rain on Fridays. D It never rains on Friday.

⬭ 2

Complete the following sentences in the best way by choosing one word from each set of brackets.

Example Tall is to (tree, <u>short</u>, colour) as narrow is to (thin, white, <u>wide</u>).

16 Drenched is to (waterless, saturated, weeping) as arid is to (stagnant, parched, overcast).

17 Current is to (flow, modern, dated) as historical is to (contemporary, period, family).

18 Bellow is to (whisper, yell, argue) as discuss is to (debate, disagree, lecture).

19 (Tennis, Riding, Running) is to (racquet, stick, ball) as cricket is to bat.

20 Car is to (passengers, windscreen, road) as (plane, bike, train) is to tracks.

⬭ 5

In a refrigerated section of a supermarket there are two shelves of goods, one above the other. From the information below, find the correct area for each type of food.

LEFT　　　　　　　　　　　　　　TOP　　　　　　　　　　　　RIGHT

A	B FRENCH CHEESE	C	D
E YOGURT	F	G	H BUTTER

BOTTOM

The cream is somewhere to the left of the fruit juice but to the right of the yogurt.

The milk is not next to either of the cheeses. It is directly under the fruit juice.

The British cheese is next to the French cheese.

The fresh pastry is at one end of the top shelf.

21 British cheese _____		**22** milk _____	
23 fresh pastry _____		**24** fruit juice _____	
25 cream _____			

5

Give the two missing pairs of letters in the following sequences. The alphabet has been written out for you.

A B C D E F G H I J K L M N O P Q R S T U V W X Y Z

Example	CQ	DP	EQ	FP	_GQ_	_HP_
26	—	FG	IJ	—	OP	RS
27	BD	—	JL	—	RT	VX
28	—	DO	—	HS	JU	LW
29	—	TE	—	VC	WB	XA
30	TC	VB	XC	ZB	—	—

5

Underline the word in the brackets closest in meaning to the word in capitals.

Example	UNHAPPY	(unkind	death	laughter	sad	friendly)
31	CONSENT	(conserve	apply	reject	believe	agree)
32	BLUSH	(embarrass	blanch	upset	redden	madden)

33	ATTAIN	(strive	utter	wonder	achieve	believe)	
34	CRINGE	(wince	pleat	satisfy	twist	avoid)	
35	QUAKE	(trouble	tribal	tremble	tragic	trivial)	5

Find the four-letter word hidden at the end of one word and the beginning of the next word in each sentence. The order of the letters may not be changed.

Example We had ba<u>ts and</u> balls.   <u>sand</u>

36 The hawk killed the young bird in my garden.   _____

37 Our class bookshelves tumbled down, making us jump.   _____

38 My broken glass shattered all over the floor.   _____

39 Her donkey has a loud bray and huge ears!   _____

40 Polar bears survive in very cold conditions.   _____   5

Underline the two words, one from each group, that are the closest in meaning.

Example (race, shop, <u>start</u>)   (finish, <u>begin</u>, end)

41 (smoothly, clumsy, skimpy)   (jumpy, lumpy, meagre)

42 (loyal, brittle, fragile)   (robust, steadfast, placid)

43 (malice, kindness, eagerness)   (spite, cruelty, outrage)

44 (dishonest, flawless, earnest)   (flawed, distinct, sincere)

45 (carcass, celebrity, journey)   (luggage, corpse, model)   5

Underline two words, one from each group, that go together to form a new word. The word in the first group always comes first.

Example (hand, <u>green</u>, for)   (light, <u>house</u>, sure)

46 (post, part, pink)   (mail, wing, man)

47 (star, bright, feet)   (stage, strike, light)

48 (be, on, deep)   (high, low, four)

49 (ship, boat, punt)   (float, time, wreck)

50 (take, sore, ball)   (foot, care, room)   5

47

Find the letter that will complete both pairs of words, ending the first word and starting the second. The same letter must be used for both pairs of words.

Example mea (<u>t</u>) able   fi (<u>t</u>) ub

51 stam (__) ick   sto (__) ea

52 ba (__) ash   pur (__) ation

53 purs (__) nd   cur (__) at

54 gan (__) row   sprin (__) rab

55 hig (__) oe   wit (__) elp

5

56 If the code for SPRING is $ ^ & * + #, what is the code for GRIP?

57 Using the same code, decode + * ^ $.

58 If the code for WINTER is g 8 4 @ > D, what is the code for TWIN?

59 Using the same code, decode D > 4 @.

A B C D E F G H I J K L M N O P Q R S T U V W X Y Z

Example If the code for CAT is D B U, what is the code for DOG?   <u>E P H</u>

60 If the code for DUCK is F W E M, what is the code for SWAN?

5

Change the first word into the last word by changing one letter at a time and making a new, different word in the middle.

Example CASE   <u>CASH</u>   LASH

61 DUST   _____   HUSK

62 COMB   _____   CORE

63 PUNY   _____   BONY

64 TOOL   _____   TILL

65 VEIN   _____   PAIN

5

Mixed paper 8

Underline the one word in each group that **cannot be made** from the letters of the word in capital letters.

Example	STATIONERY	stone	tyres	ration	<u>nation</u>	noisy
1	CENTRAL	clear	trace	crane	treat	crate
2	WINTERS	stern	swine	steer	rinse	write
3	MAGPIES	image	pages	games	ageism	spies
4	SPEAKER	spear	rakes	parks	pears	rears
5	FINGERS	sneer	grief	singe	grins	fires

5

Move one letter from the first word and add it to the second word to make two new words.

Example	hunt	sip	<u>hut</u>	<u>snip</u>
6	snack	law	_____	_____
7	knave	nit	_____	_____
8	greed	rasp	_____	_____
9	bread	spry	_____	_____
10	scale	sour	_____	_____

5

Find two words, one from each set in brackets, that will complete the sentence in the most sensible way. Underline both words.

Example Flea is to (fly, <u>flee</u>, insect) as bear is to (fur, dog, <u>bare</u>).

11 Cow is to (calf, donkey, field) as horse is to (gallop, mare, foal).

12 Insolent is to (polite, rude, silly) as honest is to (trustworthy, caring, truth).

2

If all the letters of the word KETTLES are put into alphabetical order, which comes:

13 after S? _____   14 second? _____

15 in the middle? _____

3

49

Find the four-letter word hidden at the end of one word and the beginning of the next word in each sentence. The order of the letters may not be changed.

Example We had bats <u>and</u> balls.   <u>sand</u>

16 He was delighted with all his presents.   _____

17 It rained all day and the stream overflowed.   _____

18 Bats manage to catch insects while they are flying.   _____

19 We had to put words in alphabetical order.   _____

20 Mac was pleased with his test result.   _____   **5**

A B C D E F G H I J K L M N O P Q R S T U V W X Y Z

Example If the code for CAT is D B U, what is the code for DOG?   <u>E P H</u>

21 If the code for PARK is Q B S L, what is the code for BALL? _____

22 If the code for ZIPS is X G N Q, what is the code for TONE? _____

23 If the code for DUNE is C T M D, decode E H Q L.   _____

24 If the code for POTS is Q P U T, decode T U J S.   _____

25 If the code for OWLS is L T I P, decode Y B X H.   _____   **5**

If d = 2, a = 5, c = 1, b = 12, f = 20 and e = 3, work out the answers to these calculations. Write each answer as a letter.

26 (f ÷ a) × e = _____   27 d + a + c + b = _____

28 (ae) − (cb) = _____   29 (b ÷ e) × a = _____

30 (f − b) − (d + a) = _____   **5**

Look at the first group of three words. The word in the middle has been made from the two other words. Complete the second group of three words in the same way, making a new word in the middle of the group.

Example PAIN   INTO   T<u>OO</u>K   ALSO   <u>SOON</u>   ONLY

31 MADE   DAME   TUNE   SORT   _____   JADE

32 ZIPS   SIDE   EDDY   AXLE   _____   TIDY

33 GAME   MEAN   CLAN   RATE   _____   CLAM

34 HOOD   FOOD   FLIP   COLD   _____   GREW

35 ZOOM   MOAN   HAND   POOL   _____   ROPE   **5**

(50)

Underline the one word in brackets that is most opposite in meaning to the word in capitals.

Example WIDE   (broad   vague   long   <u>narrow</u>   motorway)

36 SOOTHE   (balm   aggravate   complicate   endanger   ease)

37 JUVENILE   (elderly   childish   youngster   middle-aged   prankster)

38 GENUINE   (prime   candid   authentic   falsify   bogus)

39 SURRENDER   (yield   persevere   sympathise   act   relieve)

40 OBSCURE   (murky   opaque   indistinct   obvious   secure)

5

Change the first word into the last word by changing one letter at a time and making a new, different word in the middle.

Example CASE   <u>CASH</u>   LASH

41 HARP   _____   MARE

42 BEND   _____   BELT

43 FURY   _____   BUSY

44 KIND   _____   WAND

45 CAPE   _____   COPY

5

Rearrange the letters in capitals to make another word. The new word has something to do with the first two words or phrases.

Example spot   soil   SAINT   <u>STAIN</u>

46 pinch   take   LEAST   _____

47 to brown   browned bread   STOAT   _____

48 rise over   tall building   WROTE   _____

49 released   set loose   DEFER   _____

50 hazard   peril   GARDEN   _____

5

Six children are waiting in line for lunch.

Malek is at one end of the queue and Suki is third in line.

Hamish and Bo have 3 people between them.

Corinne stands next to and between Sue and Hamish.

51 Who stands behind Malek? _____

52 Who is last in line? _____

53 Who is fourth in line? _____

A and B like curry, C likes sausages but not curry. D likes lasagne and sausages. E only likes sausages.

54 Which is the most popular food? _____

55 Which person likes the most types of food? _____

5

Underline the two words in each line that are most similar in type or meaning.

Example	dear	pleasant	poor	extravagant	expensive
56	vanish	advance	retreat	tarnish	sully
57	thorough	caress	rigorous	jovial	miserable
58	spout	spate	spite	sport	spurt
59	revolt	deflect	divert	resort	simulate
60	neutral	acidic	fruity	tart	conserve

5

Give the two missing pairs of letters in the following sequences. The alphabet has been written out for you.

A B C D E F G H I J K L M N O P Q R S T U V W X Y Z

Example	CQ	DP	EQ	FP	GQ	HP
61	—	XO	BN	—	BL	XK
62	MM	—	OK	PJ	—	RH
63	—	QR	—	UV	WX	YZ
64	Za	—	Xc	Wd	—	Uf
65	ts	SR	rq	QP	—	—

5